CLASSIC
CHEVROLET TRUCKS

BY DON BUNN AND THE AUTO EDITORS OF CONSUMER GUIDE®

Publications International, Ltd.

ISBN-13: 978-1-4127-1686-4
ISBN-10: 1-4127-1686-1

Manufactured in China.

8 7 6 5 4 3 2 1

Library of Congress Control Number: 2009921753

Credits

Photography:

The editors would like to thank the following people and organizations for supplying the photography that made this book possible. They are listed below, along with the page number(s) of their photos.

Gary Cameron: 81; **Jim Courtney:** 86; **Roland Flessner:** 160, 161; **Thomas Glatch:** 55; **Conrad Gloos:** 111; **Sam Griffith:** 20, 22, 23, 62, 63, 86; **Don Heiny:** 89; **Bud Juneau:** 50, 51; **Dan Lyons:** 48, 80, 81; **Vince Manocchi:** 16, 17, 28, 29, 34, 53, 56, 57, 59, 71, 74, 75, 85, 87, 88, 129, 149; **Doug Mitchel:** 36, 37, 51, 70, 78, 84, 86, 87, 103, 110, 186; **Ron Moorhead:** 97; **Mike Mueller:** 14, 15; **Nina Padgett:** 18, 19; **Jay Peck:** 87, 132; **Gary Smith:** 97; **Richard Spiegelman:** 89; **Steve Statham:** 99; **Denis L. Tanney:** 55; **David Temple:** 71, 96, 130, 144, 145; **Bob Tenney:** 106, 107; **Phil Toy:** 55, 79; **W.C. Waymack:** 48, 55, 58, 72, 88, 96, 98, 99, 108, 109, 111, 115, 124, 125, 134, 136; **White Eagle Studios:** 86

Cover: Doug Mitchel; owner: David Meyer
Back Cover: Dan Lyons, Vince Manocchi, Mike Mueller, GM Media

Chapter Opener Illustrations by Frank Peiler: 6-7, 8-9, 24-25, 42-43, 64-65, 90-91, 118-119, 138-139, 154-155, 174-175

Owners:

Special thanks to the owners of the cars featured in this book for their cooperation. Their names and the page number(s) for their vehicles follow.

Richard Anderson: 72; **Orville L. Baer:** 136; **Nelson Bates:** 130; **Terry Bowman:** 111; **James and Patricia Boyk:** 86; **Willard and Evelyn Bradley:** 124, 125; **Roy and Sandi Brookshire:** 88; **Dan Brown:** 99; **Richard Carl:** 111; **David Chance:** 144, 145; **H. Curtis Cole:** 34, back cover; **Contemporary and Investment Automobiles:** 132; **Bill Cotherman:** 36, 37; **Clarence E. DeClue:** 96; **Richard DeVecchi:** 50, 51; **Joseph H. Edmonds:** 85; **Ernie's Wrecker Service:** 63; **Fairway Chevrolet:** 18, 19; **Bob H. Firth:** 106, 107; **Sam Fittante:** 71; **Stephen Foster:** 97; **Paul Garlick:** 99; **William Giembroniewicz:** 48; **Whitney and Diane Haist:** 55, 79; **William T. Hayes and sons:** 62; **Robert Ingold:** 87; **Pat and Michael Jackson:** 51; **Chesley Jacobs:** 78; **Bob Kamerer:** 111; **Bill Kaprelian:** 70; **Terry Knight:** 58; **Bill and Diann Kohley:** 78; **Jim Lanwermeyer:** 98; **Norbert C. Laubach:** 103; **Ken J. Louderman:** 87; **Raymond L. May:** 84; **David Meyer:** cover; **Danny L. Naile:** 115; **Karl Oliver:** 87; **Tom and Clara Orr:** 88; **Ralph Marano:** 89; **Herman Pfauter:** 53; **Scott Pickle:** 28, 29; **Steve Provart:** 108, 109; **Gary Romoser:** 55; **Lydia and Byron Ruetten:** 110; **Joseph F. Salierno:** 71; **Bob Schaffhauser:** 48; **Eldon Schmidt:** 59, 62; **William Schoenbeck:** 20, 22, 23; **Jerry Shumate:** 134; **Tom Slusser:** 55; **Fred A. Smith:** 129; **Tom Snively:** 14, 15, back cover; **Tom Stackhouse:** 89; **Larry and Susan Steemke:** 149; **James F. Stumpf, Jr.:** 86; **Dennis Syphrett:** 96; **William and Patricia Thomas:** 80, 81, back cover; **Bruce Valley:** 81; **Robert Warnick:** 56, 57; **Bill Wendelaar:** 55; **Bobby Wiggins:** 86; **Bob Willshire:** 97; **Daniel Wright:** 16, 17

Our appreciation to the historical archives and media services groups at General Motors Corporation.

About The Auto Editors of Consumer Guide®:

The Auto Editors of Consumer Guide® have been publishing hardcover books since 1977, including the popular *Cars of the '30s/'40s/'50s/'60s/'70s* series, numerous marque histories, and the often-referenced *Encyclopedia of American Cars*.

The editors also publish the award-winning bimonthly *Collectible Automobile®* magazine, and their new-car evaluations are featured on consumerguide.com, one of the web's most popular automotive websites that is visited by 2.5 million shoppers per month.

Contents

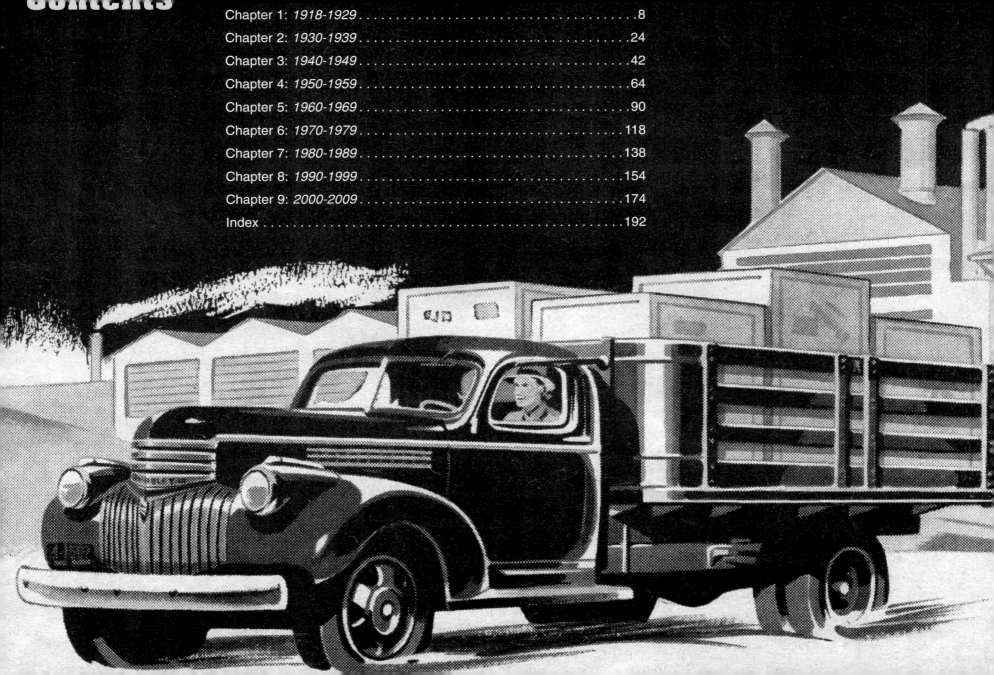

It was seven years after Chevrolet was founded that the company entered the commercial market, its first trucks being based on beefed-up car chassis. From the start, both "light-duty" ½-ton and "heavy-duty" one-ton models were offered, and that set the stage for the wide range of trucks that have since worn the Chevrolet nameplate.

Arriving in early 1918, Chevrolet's first truck was essentially the company's 490 passenger car (named for its $490 price) with stronger springs and only the hood and cowl as the "body"; the rest had to be supplied by an outside manufacturer or built by the buyer. Arriving later that same year was the one-ton Model T (sometimes called "Series T"), which was built on the chassis of Chevrolet's larger Series FA passenger car. The T was available as just a chassis with front sheetmetal, or with an open-topped body with a cargo bed in back.

What is today known as a "pickup truck"—with enclosed cab and rear cargo bed—wasn't offered direct from the Chevrolet factory until the early 1930s. Because these vehicles had such wide-ranging applications and thus appeal, they quickly became the mainstay of most companies' commercial line. Over time, these trucks became widely available in ½-, ¾-, and one-ton ratings, and other body styles, such as the station-wagon-like Panel Delivery, were often built off a company's pickup platform. These trucks have come to be known as "light-duty" commercial vehicles and traditionally make up the vast majority of sales—and collector interest. Because of that, this book primarily focuses on Chevrolet's light-duty trucks, though medium- and heavy-duty models are regularly shown as representative examples of their design generation.

Chapters cover a decade and begin with an introduction that touches on the highlights for each year. Following that are ads, brochures, original factory art, and color photos of pristine restorations that depict the wide range of vehicles offered by Chevrolet over the years that fall under the category of "trucks"—including car-based Sedan Deliverys and the classic El Camino, along with vans, minivans, and the ever-popular SUVs.

Chevrolet trucks have been on the road now for more than 90 years, and we hope you'll enjoy this tribute to the legendary workhorses that have proudly worn the blue bowtie.

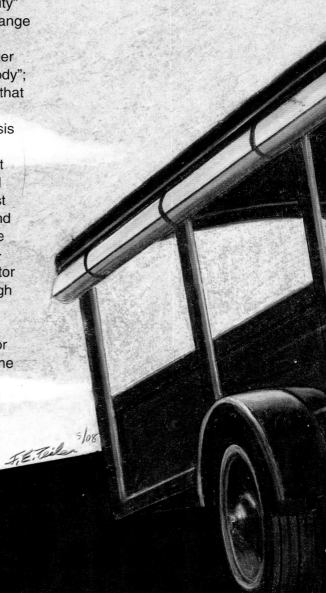

CHAPTER 1
1918-1929

When William Durant and Louis Chevrolet began selling Chevrolet cars in November 1911 for the 1912 model year, their new company was not part of General Motors. Formerly Durant was head of GM, a company he founded in 1908, but he had been forced out by the company's bankers who considered him unfit to run the business. When Durant later started the Chevrolet Motor Company on November 3, 1911, his long-term strategy was to use Chevrolet to regain control of General Motors. He reasoned he could quickly grow the new company into a very successful and profitable enterprise, which would enable him to purchase GM stock until he had a controlling interest. His inspiration was Henry Ford, whose Model T had proven successful beyond anyone's wildest dreams. Durant figured he could take on Ford with a competing low-priced car. Indeed, Chevrolets sold well enough and generated sufficient profit that by 1916, Durant controlled 54.5 percent of GM stock. He walked into GM headquarters and declared himself president.

The first Chevrolet trucks went on sale in **1918,** the same year Chevrolet Motor Company became part of GM. The light-duty trucks were based on Chevrolet's Series 490 passenger car, which had been introduced a couple of years earlier to compete directly with Ford's Model T. The 490 designation came from the car's price—$490—which was the same as that of the Model T. Ford immediately lowered the price of a Model T after the Series 490 was announced.

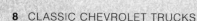

That first Chevrolet truck was called the Model 490 Light Delivery. The ½-ton-rated hauler was offered as a chassis-cowl only, meaning it included the chassis with engine, transmission, driveline, and the front sheetmetal, which comprised the hood, front fenders, grille, and headlights. A windshield was available at extra cost. Customers were expected to provide their own cab and body. In most cases, these were constructed of wood and were purchased from outside independent body companies, but some buyers built their own.

The 490's wheelbase was only 102 inches and the truck was rated for a maximum payload of 1000 pounds. Power came from a four-cylinder overhead-valve engine displacing 171 cubic inches. This engine, which initially developed 26 horsepower, lasted through the 1928 model year. The transmission was the same three-speed "stick" as used in Chevrolet cars, and the company wasn't shy about advertising its selective-gear-shift transmission against Ford's foot-pedal-operated transmission. The 490 was equipped with 30x3 ½ balloon tires front and rear, and carried a list price of $595.

The Chevrolet 490 Light Delivery Wagon had a reputation for ease of control in traffic or on the open road. Brake and clutch pedals were in just the right position, and the accelerator had a special footrest to prevent fatigue. The gearshift lever was at arm's length so as to be readily operated without changing the position of the driver's body.

Chevrolet also offered a heavy-duty truck in 1918. Called the Model T, it was based on the company's Model FA passenger-car chassis beefed up a bit for commercial service. Powered by an OHV four-cylinder engine displacing 224 cubic inches and producing 37 horsepower, it rode a 125-inch wheelbase and was rated for one-ton capacity. The Model T featured worm drive, a half-floating rear axle, 31×4 balloon front tires, 32×4 solid-rubber rear tires, eight-leaf front springs, and 12-leaf rear springs. Top speed was limited by a governor to 25 mph. Standard were electric starter and lights, a horn, and a windshield. Oddly, the headlights were mounted on the cowl rather than up near the radiator as were those on the 490, and this remained a Model T styling trademark for several years.

As a chassis-cab, the sturdily constructed Model T listed for $1325. A Flare Board Express (sort of a topless pickup truck) went for $1460, and one with a canopy top was $1545. These trucks had two compartments under the three-person bench seat; one was for the gasoline tank, the other for storage.

Competition in the heavy-hauling market was already fierce when Chevrolet began offering trucks in 1918. Ford was well established by that time, as were several smaller makes, and all still had to compete against traditional horse-drawn wagons.

Predictably, Chevrolet trucks saw few changes for **1919.** The 490 Light Delivery got an electric starter and revised spare-tire carrier, and its price jumped by $140 to $735. Meanwhile, the Model FA car that formed the basis for the Model T truck was redesignated the FB as it adopted a longer 110-inch wheelbase, but since the truck was already on a 125-inch span, that didn't affect the Model T any. Nor did it affect prices, which carried over from 1918. On a company note, rising sales put Chevrolet second only to Ford in popularity, though some lean years lay ahead.

For **1920,** the 490 received full-crowned, reverse-curve front fenders (the fenders were now arched in cross section rather than flat and flowed into the running boards with a curve rather than a crease), and the headlights were mounted directly to them rather than to a crossbar. Although Chevrolet still didn't make its own bodies, it now installed bodies made by outside manufacturers on the production line so buyers didn't have to add them separately. These included an express (pickup) body with a driver's seat and top, along with the same that featured two more rows of seats for passenger use. The Model T carried over virtually unchanged, though pneumatic tires replaced solid ones at the rear. Prices for the 490 dropped a bit, while those for the Model T held the course. Despite recent sales successes at Chevrolet, GM began floundering under a mountain of debt and unsold cars, and Durant was pressured to resign as

president of General Motors, never to return.

A new truck was added between the 490 and the Model T for **1921,** but it would have a short life. Listed as a ¾-ton, the Model G carried the front sheetmetal of the 490 but the engine of the Model T. Prices started at $920 for a bare chassis, running to $1095 for a canopy express. The 490 and Model T carried on with few changes. By this time, Chevrolet had fallen to a disappointing fifth in the sales race.

For **1922,** the ¾-ton Model G swapped its 224-cid Model T engine for the 171-cid unit from the 490, but other changes for all three models were minor. However, prices were dropped to spur sales, with the 490 starting at $510, the Model G at $745, and the Model T at $1125.

Chevrolet's passenger cars took on the Superior name for **1923,** and so did the trucks. Visual alterations included a raised hood line and a taller, flatter-topped radiator. For the first time, all trucks carried the same basic styling. This represented a greater leap for the one-ton model, which previously looked more primitive. The ½-ton truck was called the Superior Series A, though some midyear changes—including a curved front axle—brought with them the Series B moniker. One-ton models were labeled Series D. The ¾-ton truck, previously called the Model G, was dropped. Surprisingly, the A, B, and D all shared the same 171-cid engine previously used in the lighter-duty models. However, the D had heavy-duty underpinnings and a longer wheelbase: 120 inches (125 available) vs. 103.

Half-ton versions entered the **1924** model year again carrying the Series B label, but were called Series F after reverting to a straight front axle midyear. One-tons likewise changed names midway through the model year—from Series D to Series H—though there were few changes.

The ½-ton Series F and one-ton Series H continued into the **1925** model year that began in fall 1924, but were replaced in January 1925 by revised Series K and Series M models, respectively. Half-ton Series K models had Fisher-built bodies offering a vertical ventilating windshield and introduced a modern single-plate dry-disc clutch to replace the traditional cone clutch. It was during this period that Chevrolet sales began rebounding strongly, enough so that they would surpass Ford's within a couple of years.

Yet another midyear name change effectively split the **1926** model offerings. At the start of the model year, the ½-ton Series K had its headlights moved to a crossbar rather than being mounted directly to the fenders—a seemingly regressive step, as they had resided on a crossbar from 1918 through 1919 before moving to the fenders—but mechanical changes arriving in January 1926 were sufficient to prompt a new Series V designation. These included wider brakes and a belt-driven (rather than gear-driven) generator. Also new was the Roadster Pickup, essentially a regular car with a small pickup bed in back in place of the rumble seat.

Meanwhile, the one-ton trucks got two name changes during the model year. What had been the 1925 Series M became the 1926 Series R at the start of the year as it gained four inches in wheelbase (to 124). The Series R was superseded midyear by the Series X, which carried the modern front sheetmetal of Chevrolet's contemporary Series K cars, along with offering the company's first production truck body with an enclosed, all-steel cab.

Series V half-tons carried into the **1927** model year with a few revisions, but a restyled truck appeared midyear with a whole new designation that once again mirrored the similarly changed car line. The Capitol AA Series AA sported a dipped-center radiator shell and bullet-shaped headlights, but retained the half-tonner's tried-and-true mechanicals.

Ditto for one-ton trucks. The Series X carried into the 1927 model year virtually unchanged, then switched to the Capitol AA Series LM nomenclature as it adopted the same styling changes as the ½-ton Series AA.

Late 1927 models of both the ½-ton and one-ton trucks carried over into early **1928,** but once again, revised versions arrived midyear. In the case of the ½-ton models, they came with a new model name that corresponded to those used on Chevrolet's cars: National AB. They also got the Series AB tag. These ½-ton trucks added front brakes (formerly rear only) and four inches in wheelbase (now 107).

One-ton models that arrived midyear continued with their

Capitol model name but now with an AB (rather than AA) suffix. They started out as the Series LO, then became the Series LP as they adopted a standard four-speed transmission. All of Chevrolet's trucks continued to be powered by the 171-cid four-cylinder engine in use since 1918, but not for much longer.

Chevrolet set a new standard for truck power when it introduced the light-truck industry's first overhead-valve six-cylinder engine in **1929.** Because a truck's purpose is to move the largest possible load in the shortest possible time at the lowest possible cost, Chevrolet engineers hit a grand slam with their new 194-cubic-inch, 46-horsepower "Cast-Iron Wonder" engine. Still of overhead-valve configuration, the six provided a great increase in power and torque over the old four (which, by the end of its life, produced 35 horsepower) and allowed Chevrolet trucks to move heavier loads faster than in the past. Chevrolet's advertising program was brilliant, as it promoted "A six for the price of four." Features of the new six included cast-iron pistons, an efficient cooling system, and a non-pressurized engine lubrication system. Ford answered with a flathead V-8 in 1932 and Dodge with a flathead six in 1933, but this engine gave Chevrolet trucks a big boost in performance—and sales—until then.

The new six-cylinder-powered ½-ton truck wore the International AC Series AC label. Styling alterations included a square-up radiator and vertical side vents only at the rear of the hood. A floor-mounted button allowed drivers to change the angle of the headlights slightly, effectively giving "high" and "low" beams. The Series AC Light Delivery was rated for a maximum payload of 1000 pounds. It was equipped with rear fenders and a spare rim for only $400—less than the four-cylinder 1928 ½-ton. The six's higher speeds allowed delivery men and salesmen to make more stops per day than was possible with the slower four-cylinder trucks. A $595 Sedan Delivery with a body by the Geneva Body Company was a new model. All Chevrolet trucks for 1929 featured new steel disc wheels; wooden wheels had gone the way of the buggy whip.

The new six enabled Chevrolet to upgrade its one-ton model to a 1½-ton truck. The new International AC Series was offered either with or without a cab, but as before, no factory-built bodies were available.

With its new six-cylinder engine, good reputation, and attractive prices, Chevrolet was poised to enter the 1930s in fine fettle. Unfortunately, a stock market crash on October 29, 1929, triggered the Great Depression, which would bring ruin to many companies and severely challenge those that survived.

Chevrolet's first commercial vehicles debuted for 1918, the same year the company officially became a part of General Motors. Like other manufacturers of the day, Chevrolet built only the complete chassis and cowl, leaving the bodywork to various commercial coachbuilding firms. The Model 490 Light Delivery chassis sold for $595—body not included. This 490 pickup illustrates the ratio of Chevrolet/outside supplier components clearly—the wooden portion of the truck is the part Chevy didn't furnish. The Light Delivery chassis was mostly shared with Chevrolet's passenger cars but was fitted with heavier springs that enabled it to handle a payload of 1000 pounds. The engine—a 171 cubic-inch four-cylinder rated at 26 horsepower—was also shared with the 490 passenger-car lineup. Chevrolet's first one-ton truck, ironically dubbed Model T, also joined the roster this year. It used modified mechanics from Chevy's upscale Model FA passenger car.

The popular 490 series of vehicles was little changed for 1919, though the Light Delivery got an electric starter. This restored beauty is equipped with an accessory water-temperature gauge atop the radiator, a period device generally known as a "Moto-Meter." (Moto-Meters bearing the Chevrolet trademark weren't offered until 1923, however.) The cargo area featured a drop-down tailgate, along with curtains for semi-secure hauling. Note also the roof-mounted turn signals, caged dome light, and the hand-operated horn nestled next to the driver's seat behind the spare tire. As ever, the 490's little four-cylinder engine wasn't much for speed; rugged reliability and easy maintenance counted for a lot more in those days, and these Chevrolets delivered.

Chevrolet introduced its Superior Series K models in January 1925. Among the many mechanical improvements was a completely revised engine with a newly designed block, heavier crankshaft, and drop-forged connecting rods with larger bearings. This Series K Light Delivery has been fitted with a "C-cab" panel body, a style that was becoming a bit outdated by the mid Twenties. Instrumentation on all Series K Superiors was small and centrally grouped. As the year wore on, spark and throttle controls in the cars were moved to the dash, but trucks retained these levers on the steering column.

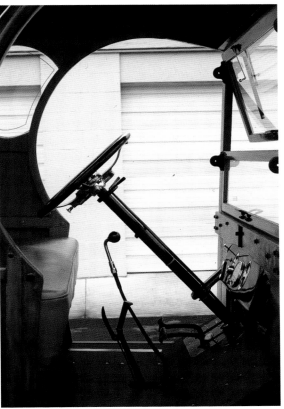

By 1928, the Chevrolet truck light-duty line—now dubbed National AB—had grown to a 107-inch wheelbase. Four-wheel brakes (still mechanical) were now standard; previous models had brakes only at the rear. Wood-spoke wheels were still common on '28 Chevy trucks, but they would soon be phased out entirely in favor of steel disc or wire wheels. Chevrolet enjoyed a particularly successful year in 1928, as Ford production was disrupted by the changeover to the Model A. The ad shown here touted Chevrolet economy and reliability while showcasing the company's commercial offerings.

The
Lowest Ton-Mile Cost
provided by
Chevrolet Trucks *at Amazing Low Prices*

LIGHT
DELIVERY
$375
(Chassis Only)
f. o. b. Flint, Mich.

UTILITY
TRUCK
$495
(Chassis Only)
f. o. b. Flint, Mich.

By removing the rear deck and installing an inexpensive slip-on box, the Chevrolet Roadster can easily be converted into a speedy and economical light delivery unit that is ideal for marketing, hauling feed, transporting tools, etc. The slip-on box can be supplied by any Chevrolet dealer.

The ROADSTER
$495
(Box extra)
f. o. b. Flint, Mich.

Powered by a valve-in-head motor that is famous the world over for its amazing endurance and efficiency ... built with a margin of over-strength in every unit ... and incorporating the most advanced engineering design throughout—Chevrolet trucks have repeatedly demonstrated their ability to deliver the world's lowest ton-mile cost!

For Every Line of Business

This matchless economy has been experienced by users in every line of business and under every condition of road and load. Merchants, manufacturers, contractors, farmers and many other users have learned that no other haulage unit does its job so satisfactorily at such low cost.

The Chevrolet Motor Company has always believed that low ton-mile cost is a fundamental requirement in commercial transportation—and every advancement in the design and construction of Chevrolet trucks has been made in the interest of economy ... to provide longer life, greater dependability and more efficient operation.

Rugged Construction

Inspect a Chevrolet truck chassis—and you will instantly see how adherence to this principle has influenced Chevrolet design. The banjo-type rear axle is big and sturdy—built to stand up indefinitely under every condition of usage. The frame is constructed of heavy channel steel, rigidly reenforced

to withstand the twisting and weaving strains of rough roads. And the long semi-elliptic springs are extra-leaved to cradle the heaviest loads over every type of highway. Furthermore, the benefits of great volume production and scientific management have been utilized to make the first cost as low as possible—a fact that is strikingly demonstrated in the amazing low prices of today's Chevrolet trucks.

Trial-Load Demonstration

Your Chevrolet dealer can provide a body type designed especially for your business and will gladly arrange a trial-load demonstration. See him today.

CHEVROLET MOTOR COMPANY, DETROIT, MICHIGAN
Division of General Motors Corporation

QUALITY AT LOW COST   QUALITY AT LOW COST

This meticulously restored 1928 1/2-ton National AB pickup wears a body crafted to match the ones produced by the York-Hoover Body Corporation of Pennsylvania. Though the external facing of the body is .040-inch steel, the underlying structure is all wood. The sliding rear window, spare tire mounted at the back of the cab, and integrated bed/cab layout are all unique features of the York-Hoover body design. The 35-hp four-banger could push the pickup to a top speed of about 30 mph. Note the prominent fan shroud; one bit of evidence that the new longer-wheelbase chassis was designed to accept the "Stovebolt-Six" engine that would debut for 1929.

CHAPTER 2
1930–1939

Triggered by the stock market crash of October 29, 1929, the Great Depression that followed took its toll on virtually all manufacturers, but Chevrolet weathered the storm better than most. While Chevrolet truck sales dropped from about 161,000 for calendar-year 1929 to about 118,000 for 1930, those numbers are a bit misleading, as the former represents a strong increase over the previous year thanks to the debut of the six-cylinder engine. Production in 1928—the final year for the original four-cylinder engine—was roughly 134,000, which is perhaps a more reasonable comparative figure. Sales were down to be sure—and would go lower—but Chevrolet trucks were still popular.

After introduction of the groundbreaking six-cylinder engine for 1929, Chevrolet trucks got little new for **1930** besides a revised instrument panel pirated from the company's car line and a new name: the Universal. They continued in ½-ton (Series AD) and 1½-ton (Series LR) versions, both powered by the 46-horsepower, 194-cubic-inch six that had set the truck world on its ear.

As had been the case since the beginning, most commercial bodies fitted to Chevrolet trucks were built by outside manufacturers, whether installed by the factory, the dealership, or the buyers themselves. The only commercial body built by Chevrolet for 1930 was the ½-ton Sedan Delivery, which was essentially the automotive two-door Coach with blanked-out rear side windows. Prices that had already dropped for 1929 dropped further for 1930 in response to the Depression. The ½-ton chassis now started at $365 ($35 less than in '29), while the 1½-ton chassis went for $520 (down $25). Remaining at $595 was the Sedan Delivery—odd, since its automotive Coach counterpart, which included a rear seat and side windows, was discounted to $565.

The Independence Series of **1931** Chevrolet trucks was historically significant in that it debuted the factory-built Chevrolet pickup. Also that year, the ½-ton wheelbase increased from 107 inches to 109, and the 1½-ton Utility trucks were offered in two wheelbases—131 and 157 inches—with single or dual rear wheels. Other changes included louvers that stretched farther along the sides of the hood and a horsepower increase from 46 to 50.

A new ½-ton chassis with open cab and pickup box cost only $440. It was one of four commercial bodies Chevrolet offered for 1931, the others being a panel truck, sedan delivery, and canopy. The cab was redesigned with a one-piece steel roof; at last the former structure of wood and fabric was history. The cab was wider and the seats were also wider and more comfortable, the doors were considerably larger for easier entry, and a rubber floor mat was furnished. Sales dropped to just below 100,000 units.

Significant changes for the **1932** Confederate Series BB trucks were the inclusion of a silent-synchromesh transmission and a switch from an automobile engine to an engine built specifically for trucks. Still displacing 194 cubic inches, horsepower was up to 53 at 2800 rpm from 50 at 2600 rpm and maximum torque jumped by seven pound-feet to 131 at 800 rpm. Half-ton models switched from 19-inch steel disc wheels to 18-inch wire wheels. It was the first year that Chevrolet truck styling didn't correspond to the company's car styling save for the car-based Sedan Delivery. Cars were mildly updated, but trucks retained their 1931 look. Truck sales plummeted to about 66,000 as the Depression bottomed out.

The Eagle/Master Eagle Series CB of **1933** would be the last Chevrolet truck to use a series name as well as a series designation. Power rose once again as the engine's displacement was boosted to 207 cubic inches with an attendant increase in horsepower to 56 at 2750 rpm and maximum torque to 146 lb-ft. A four-speed transmission was newly optional in place of the standard three-speed. Sedan Deliveries remained commercial versions of the automotive Coach model, while other trucks adopted styling similar to the 1932 car line. Sales rebounded to just under 100,000 units, giving Chevrolet nearly half the light-truck market.

The new **1934** Chevrolet Series DB Master Commercial truck line was completely restyled. For the first time, trucks didn't share front-end sheetmetal with Chevrolet cars, except for the Sedan Delivery, which was no longer considered part of the Light Delivery truck line. Truck cabs were larger and more comfortable. Wheelbase grew from 109 to 112. Body offerings remained at three: canopy, panel, and pickup.

The 1934 trucks became the **1935** Series EB Master Commercial models with very little change except for a horsepower bump from 56 to 60. New was the Carryall Suburban, an all-steel eight-passenger station wagon. The car-based Sedan Delivery now came in two lengths: the EC on a 107-inch wheelbase and the EA on a 113-inch span.

Though neither was considered a "truck" by this time, the Sedan Delivery was joined by a Coupe Delivery for **1936;** it looked like a traditional coupe, but with a short bed sticking out the back in place of a trunklid. Early 1936 Chevrolet Series FB Master Commercial models featured some noteworthy changes, including hydraulic brakes on ½-ton models and instruments grouped in front of the driver instead of in the center of the dash, but the basic truck carried over from 1935. At midyear, a new cab arrived that was two inches lower with more rounded styling, and 1½-ton models adopted the hydraulic brakes of their lighter brothers. Although displacement remained at 207 cubic inches, the engine got a significant boost to 79 horsepower. The combination of an improving economy, pent-up demand, and strong products helped Chevrolet truck sales reach an impressive 204,000 units, up from 167,000 in 1935.

Chevrolet trucks returned to using car front sheetmetal for **1937** and looked all the more modern for it. New were ¾- and one-ton models to fill the load gap between the existing ½-ton and 1½-ton trucks. All carried a larger engine, now displacing 216 cubic inches and rated at 85 horsepower. New for '37 was a ½-ton walk-in delivery truck.

The **1938** models were little changed save for a more modern looking wraparound grille and minor revisions to the hood vents. Added were ¾- and one-ton panel trucks and walk-in delivery trucks.

The **1939** Chevrolet truck line received restyled front sheetmetal and a new cab with split vee'd windshield. The cab was designed for driver comfort and convenience, with more headroom, a wider seat, and a more attractive and functional instrument panel. All 1939 trucks had longer wheelbases: 113½ inches for the ½-ton: 123¾ inches for the ¾- and one-tons, and 133 and 158½ inches for the heavy models.

The car-based Sedan Delivery and Coupe Delivery returned, now with a steering-column-mounted shift lever instead of a floor-mounted one. At the opposite end of the spectrum, Chevrolet added a pug-nosed Cab-Over-Engine (COE) version of its 1½-ton truck. Its shorter length and tighter turning radius made it popular for inner-city work.

As the 1930s progressed, a recovering economy sparked a dramatic truck sales race between Chevrolet and Ford. Until 1939, Ford had enjoyed first place five times during the decade and led—barely—in total units sold: 1,247,081 to Chevrolet's 1,210,650. In 1939, however, Chevrolet won the annual sales race, and would continue to do so for the next 30 years.

The $400 Series AD roadster delivery was the spunkiest member of Chevrolet's 1930 truck lineup. It was powered by the 194-cid ohv inline six—the "Cast-Iron Wonder"—that Chevrolet had introduced for 1929, though stated horsepower was now up to 50 (from an introductory 46) at 2600 rpm. A new instrument panel featured round, dark-faced dials. Many body parts were shared with Chevrolet's passenger-car roadster, including the hood, fenders, cowl, doors, and a painted version of the passenger cars' grille shell. Pickup beds, however, were made by several manufacturers. Among them was Martin-Parry, which General Motors purchased in late 1930, guaranteeing its own supply of these units in the future. Despite tough economic times and slumping production, Chevrolet built its 7-millionth vehicle this year.

CHEVROLET
PICK-UP TRUCKS

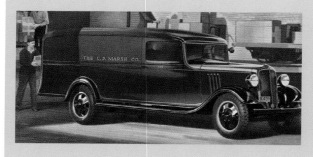

1932

The 1932 Chevrolet trucks were the first to wear styling distinct from the company's passenger-car models. Half-ton pickups like the ones shown here came with both open and closed-cab bodies; the latter included an electric windshield wiper and a cowl vent for cabin ventilation. The available all-metal canopy top slotted into the pickup bed's stake pockets and featured "weatherproof" pull-down curtains at the sides and rear. The pickup bed itself was a bit small by modern standards; it measured a mere 66 inches long, 45 inches wide, and 13 inches deep. The 194-cid six got a 3-hp bump to 53 this year, and was connected to a new three-speed "Synchro-Mesh" transmission that enabled quieter, grind-free shifts.

CHEVROLET TRUCKS

1934 After a round of relatively minor changes for 1933, the Chevrolet truck line was completely restyled with its own unique sheetmetal for 1934. As before, ½-ton trucks wore 18-inch wire wheels while 1½-ton models wore heavy-duty 19-inch steel wheels. Plenty of Chevrolet-built body configurations were offered. In addition to the expected pickup, panel delivery, and stake-bed body styles, both ½-ton and 1½-ton trucks were available in a unique "canopy express" body style—essentially a panel delivery with a drop-down tailgate, open-air sides, and roll-down storm curtains. As the image at left illustrates, the new pickup cab was roomier and more comfortable than before. The simple instrument panel included a speedometer, oil gauge, water temperature gauge, ammeter, and gas gauge.

1935 No major changes were ordained for the 1935 models. Unlike other Chevrolet commercial vehicles, the Sedan Delivery (middle) was based on the passenger-car chassis. A Sedan Delivery was perfect for light work like hauling flowers, but heavier cargo demanded heavier machinery, such as the 1½-ton stake truck (above). It rode a 131-inch wheelbase and boasted 60 square feet of load space on its roomy platform.

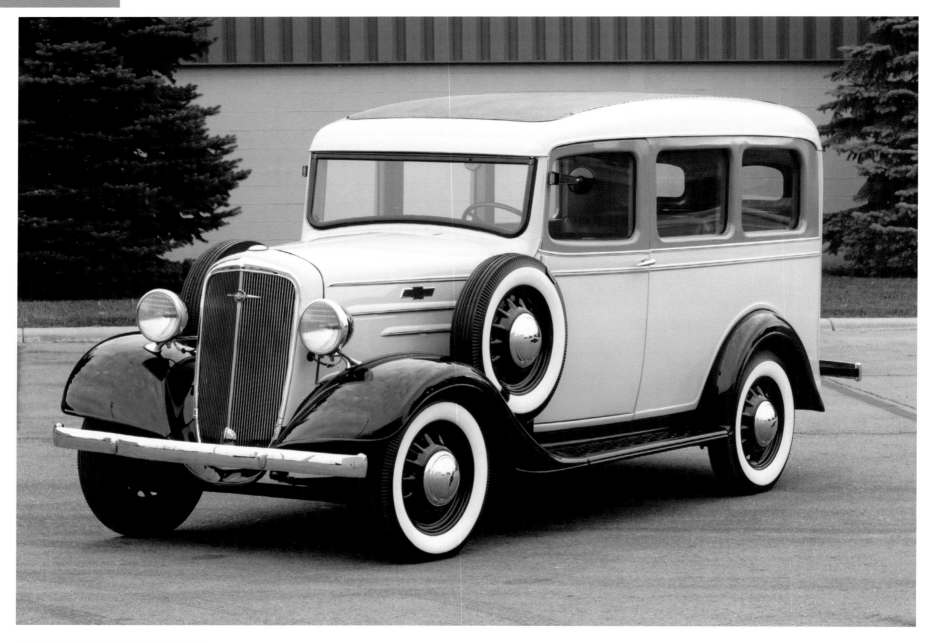

The Suburban Carryall wagon debuted for 1935 and was carried over into 1936 with minor changes. At $685, it was the priciest of Chevrolet's ½-ton models. Eight-passenger seating was standard, though accessing the rear seats through the two front doors or the dual rear doors must have been tricky. The Suburban was an innovative vehicle; it was one of the first all-steel station wagons and is sometimes credited as "the first SUV," though that term would not appear for another 50 or so years. All 1936 Chevrolet trucks got new dashboards with a glovebox and relocated instruments (they were now positioned in front of the driver instead of the center of the dash). A mild exterior facelift included a revised grille and hood sides, and fenders with slightly "skirted" sides.

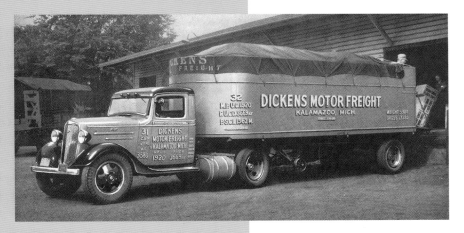

"Chevrolet Perfected Hydraulic Brakes" were the big news mechanically for the 1936 Chevrolet lineup; both trucks and cars got them. This ½-ton Panel Delivery (opposite) wears the optional stamped-steel "artillery" wheels that were being phased in to gradually replace wire wheels. The Panel Delivery rode a 112-inch wheelbase and started at $565. Its Canopy Express sibling, with open-air sides and roll-down curtains, started at $12 more. Both had a 115-cubic-foot storage capacity. The 1½-ton Chevrolet trucks still offered plenty of variety; Canopy (top left) and Open Express (top right) models rode a 131-inch wheelbase, while the stakebed model (above left) rode a 157-inch span. Chevrolet also offered 1½-ton truck chassis (above right) for tractor-trailer hauling.

Midway through the 1936 season, Chevrolet pickups got new cabs with one-piece, all-steel construction and lower, more rounded styling. A single sidemount spare tire was an oft-seen option. The trustworthy Chevrolet six remained at 207 cubic inches, but was upgraded to produce 79 horse-power, up from 60. Improvements included a new down-draft car-buretor, reworked camshaft, and full-length water jackets around the cylinders for improved cooling. The "clear-vison" instrument panel was handsome in its simplicity, as was the rest of the truck. Significantly more-modern styling, with a stream-lined, art-deco look borrowed from the passenger car line, was on the way for 1937.

The redesigned 1937 Chevrolet trucks wore up-to-the-minute "Diamond Crown" styling highlighted by plump new fenders, stream-lined headlight pods, and a shapely "waterfall" grille. The "Blue Flame" six grew to 216 cubic inches and now put out 85 horsepower and 170 lb-ft of torque. Stronger, heavier, stiffer frames featured a new "monorail" spare-tire carrier that held the spare securely in between the frame rails at the rear of the vehicle—side-mount spares were fast becoming a thing of the past. The Commercial Panel (above) wore a swoopy all-steel body on its 112-inch wheelbase. For a base price of $605, Panel buyers got an enclosed load space that was 86 inches long, 54 inches wide, and 51 inches high. The 1½-ton stake truck (opposite page, top) could be had with a 131½-inch wheelbase or a 157-inch span.

CHEVROLET COMMERCIAL PICK-UP—112-inch Wheelbase

Loading space has been increased to 77 inches by 45¾ inches. Height to top of flare boards, 16 inches. Bodies are dipped to prevent rusting. Shock absorbers are regular equipment. This model, with its streamlined cab, combines speedy, economical and efficient commercial car bodies with passenger car appearance.

CHEVROLET CARRY-ALL SUBURBAN—112-inch Wheelbase

Here's an ideal unit for use for passengers or, alternatively, for transporting varied loads. Large tires, shock absorbers, and upholstered seats complete the comfortable car. The seats are readily removed.

CHEVROLET SEDAN DELIVERY

The strikingly good-looking unit is mounted on the 1937 Master passenger car chassis, assuring easy riding, quick deliveries, and economy. Body is all-steel. Load space measures 68½ inches long, 54 inches wide, 41 inches high.

CHEVROLET COUPE PICK-UP

This most useful unit is a Master or Master De Luxe passenger car business coupe body with its pick-up box in the rear. It is furnished with a rear deck lid, by which it can be converted into a coupe. The load space is 66¼ inches long, 38⅞ inches wide, and 12¼ inches high to the top of the flare boards.

CHEVROLET 1½-TON STAKE—157-inch Wheelbase

This type of truck is available on either the 157-inch or the 131½-inch wheelbase. The stake sides are firmly aligned in durable stake pockets strongly braced and reinforced. The side stakes remain in line when the rear gate is left off. A tail gate, replacing the stake section, is furnished as optional equipment on the 157-inch model at slight added cost. The center line of the body is well ahead of the rear axle, effecting improved load distribution. The body for the 157-inch wheelbase is 81⅝ inches wide, 141½ inches long, 41¾ inches high. The body for the 131½-inch wheelbase is 81⅝ inches wide, 105½ inches long, 41¾ inches high.

CHEVROLET 1½-TON PICK-UP—131½-inch Wheelbase

The open express body, or pick-up, on the 1½-ton chassis, is a vehicle of innumerable uses and of universal application. With its new all-steel cab, it brings stylish appearance to this strictly commercial vehicle. The load space is 108 inches long, 45¾ inches wide, 19⅞ inches high to the top of the flare boards.

CHEVROLET 1½-TON STOCK RACK—157-inch Wheelbase

This model has completely improved load distribution (the same as in the 157-inch stake body). Its end gate now opens horizontally, instead of swinging on vertical fasteners. Loading of stock is facilitated and added safety is gained by this new arrangement. The load space is 141½ inches long, 81⅝ inches wide, 66 inches high.

CHEVROLET 1½-TON TRUCK—for Trailer Operation

The Chevrolet 1½-ton chassis, because of its higher power and its unusual ability to maintain full pulling power over a wide range of speeds, is especially well fitted for use with semi-trailer.

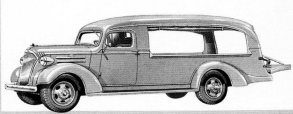

CHEVROLET 1½-TON CANOPY EXPRESS—131½-inch Wheelbase

This model combines fine appearance with rugged construction and money-making load capacity. Roll curtains protect the load in bad weather. Screen sides are available at small additional cost, protecting merchandise from theft. The load space is 110⅞ inches long, 55¼ inches wide, 53¼ inches high.

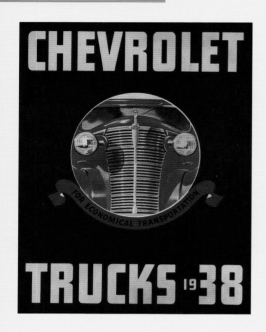

A minor facelift for 1938 included new hood side panels and a wraparound horizontal-bar grille. The cornucopia of body styles continued, and included everything from a Master Coupe pickup (which was simply a Master Coupe passenger car with the trunklid removed and replaced with a slot-in abbreviated pickup bed) to a super-stretched 201-inch-wheelbase chassis designed for use with aftermarket school-bus bodies (some of which boasted fabulous art-deco styling complete with rear fender skirts). The specialized body configurations enabled the basic Chevrolet truck architecture to be adapted to a wide variety of tasks; for example, the high-sided stake bed of the 1½-ton stock rack truck (opposite page, top right) was designed to haul livestock. An unexpected recession caused sales to drop again, to about 120,000 units, but Chevrolet still topped the industry.

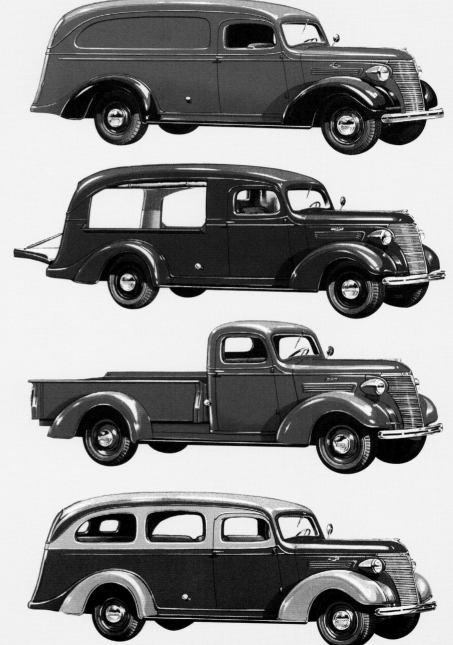

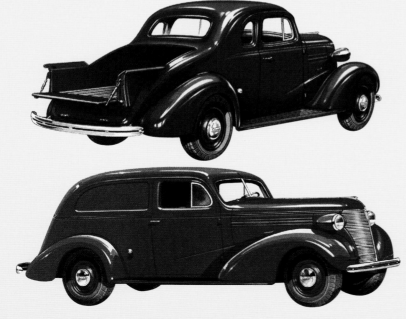

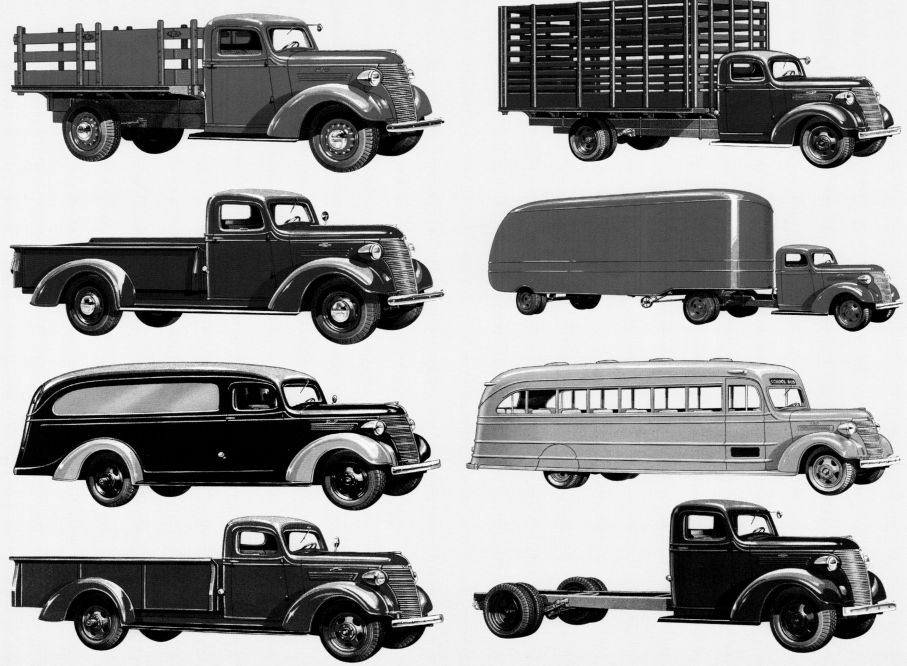

CHAPTER 3
1940-1949

With the Depression still a vivid memory as the 1940s dawned, there were already storm clouds brewing that would erupt in further challenges as the decade progressed.

Chevrolet was by now firmly entrenched as the number one selling truck in America, and those trucks didn't change much for **1940.** Most obvious was a larger nameplate positioned at the top of the grille that effectively deleted the upper-most grille bar. In addition, 1940 models featured sealed-beam headlights flanked by streamlined parking lights moved to the tops of the front fenders.

By contrast, the Sedan Delivery and Coupe Delivery adopted the all-new styling of the cars on which they were based. Wheelbases grew from 112¼ inches to an even 113, and both Master 85 and Master Deluxe versions could be ordered with Knee Action independent front suspension. Nonetheless, these car-based models remained sales slugs, accounting for just over 3100 units combined.

During **1941,** the threat of war caused consumers to purchase motor vehicles like never

before, helping set new sales records in both the United States and Canada. Truck production for military use also contributed heavily to the count. Chevrolet broke its own sales record by producing nearly 213,000 units, one-third of total industry truck sales. Arch-rival Ford was a distant second at just over 174,000.

Styling changes for '41 aimed at creating a massive look. New front fenders completely eliminated the previous fender valleys. A wide, toothy, "waterfall" grille added visual width, as did headlights moved outboard and inset into the tops of the fenders. More grille bars—horizontal this time—graced the leading edge of the hood, and when plated in chrome, the grille bars and bumper combined for a very bright nose. Chevrolet retained this basic styling until the Advance Design models were launched in 1947. Also for 1941, the engine—still displacing 216 cubic inches—was boosted from 85 to 90 horsepower.

The new ½-ton was built on a 115-inch wheelbase, the two-inch stretch allowing for additional legroom and a more inclined seatback angle for greater comfort. Body offerings included a pickup, panel, canopy, and Suburban. The ¾-ton had a 125¼-inch wheelbase and included a pickup, platform, and stake and panel bodies. However, a longer version of the panel was added on the 134½-inch chassis of the 1½-ton trucks.

The Sedan Delivery again rode a passenger-car chassis and benefited from the car line's new styling—often consid-

ered the best of its era. The wheelbase was stretched to 116 inches. Special futures included Knee Action front suspension, hydraulic shocks front and rear, and vacuum-powered gearshift. The slow-selling Coupe Pickup (formerly called the Coupe Delivery) was again available based on this same chassis.

The **1942** Chevrolet pickups were essentially unchanged from 1941. After the United States entered World War II in December 1941, government restrictions on the use of chromium resulted in what were called "blackout" models, in which most trim that was normally chrome plated was instead painted. Then the government halted normal civilian truck production early in 1942; Chevrolet ceased regular civilian production at the end of January. Some civilian models were built during the war, but they were relatively few in number.

At the onset of World War II, Chevrolet converted most of its factories to the production of war materiel. In addition to the expected military cars and trucks—of which Chevrolet built about half a million—the company made 60,000 Pratt and Whitney aircraft engines, wing sections and fuselage components for the Grumman Aircraft Company, and two thousand 90-mm guns. It also supplied 200 million pounds of aluminum forgings, 5.7 million pounds of magnesium castings, and two billion pounds of grey iron castings.

Chevrolet resumed production of civilian trucks for the general market on September 1, 1945. They were advertised as the nation's "Most Popular Pickup Truck," and were basically the same as the 1942 models save for a few engineering improvements.

Chevrolet brought to market a full line (100 models on nine wheelbases) of light, medium, and heavy-duty trucks on May 1, **1946,** complete with chrome trim. All prewar models except the Coupe Pickup—which was dropped—were now in full production. They were built for a year before 1947's Advance-Design trucks were introduced.

It's been questioned as to why Chevrolet (and Ford, for that matter) developed new truck lines before restyling their cars. According to Chevrolet sources, the reason was that the government had allowed the company to keep building civilian trucks (at a trickle of non-wartime production) on the same line as the military trucks in order to fill serious domestic truck needs and avert a crippling shortage of trucks when the war ended. Because Chevrolet didn't have to convert its production lines back to trucks after VJ Day, plans for redesigned trucks were started sooner than those for cars.

All-new styling was the big news surrounding **1947**'s Advance-Design trucks. Chevrolet believed that appearance was becoming a more important consideration to truck owners, especially to fleet operators. Buyers wanted a good-looking truck for its advertising value and to contribute to their business prestige. But at the same time, the trucks had to be practical, with no sacrifice in utility or cost of operation.

Chevrolet interviewed truck owners nationwide prior to engineering the Advance-Design series. The survey showed that larger, roomier cabs were at the top of the wish list, so Advance-Design cabs were eight inches wider and seven inches longer. The survey also called for better visibility and greater comfort. Chevrolet responded with a new seat that adjusted on an incline so that it raised and tilted as it moved forward to provide the proper seating posture, whatever the driver's height.

As the truck line expanded, it became difficult for one design to fit both light- and heavy-duty models. Thus, Chevrolet divided its 1947 truck line into the light-duty Thriftmaster and heavy-duty Loadmaster series. Though the same cab was used for both, each had a separate set of front appearance parts from the cowl forward. The two groups were styled alike to maintain an instantly recognized family resemblance, but were scaled to different proportions. Chevrolet called this approach Load Proportioned styling.

On heavy-duty Loadmasters, a body-colored gravel guard was inserted between the bumper and the grille to improve the frontal appearance by covering the bumper braces. It also prevented gravel, mud, dirt, water, and snow from being splashed onto the truck's grille.

Speaking of grilles, those for the two series looked similar but were not interchangeable. Both consisted of five parallel bars mounted horizontally to emphasize the wider cab. For the Loadmaster series, the grille was slightly taller than on the light-duty trucks, accomplished by making the bars thicker and spacing them a little farther apart. On both series, the Chevrolet name and emblem were now combined into a large plate located just above the grille. In standard trim, the grille bars were painted the same color as the rest of the truck and striped to enhance their appearance. Thriftmasters offered chrome-plated bars as an extra-cost option.

The front fenders were also proportioned to the size of the truck. Although the general design was the same, Loadmaster front fenders had larger wheel openings to accommodate the higher wheels and tires and to blend in with the taller grille. Fenders were now painted body color rather than black as they had been in 1946 and earlier, and the headlights were mounted in, not on top of the fenders.

The Deluxe panel trucks carried fender moldings that set them apart from the rest of the Advance-Design lineup. On this model, the front fenders were decorated with four horizontal chrome bars while the rear fenders carried three bars.

The hood assembly was changed from the side-opening butterfly style to a front-opening alligator type that allowed for easier engine access. Different hoods were provided for the two series, those for the Loadmaster being higher, flatter in the crown, and longer. Trim on both series consisted of the nameplate and identification plates bearing the Chevrolet name and the series—Loadmaster or Thriftmaster—on the sides of the hood.

The new doors were also larger in every dimension. They extended beyond the cab floor at the bottom to cover the exposed sills, and were four inches longer for easier entry and exit. Also, hinges were concealed for a sleeker look. In pickup tradition, only one door lock was provided, and it was on the curb side.

A broader, taller windshield was slanted at a greater angle, improving vision and adding to the truck's appearance. It was also stationary, which allowed the windshield wipers to be mounted below the glass where they looked better and worked more efficiently.

One of the most attractive features of the Advance-Design trucks was the rear quarter windows, an extra-cost option on any cab and included in the Deluxe Cab package. With the larger regular windows and added rear quarter windows, total glass area increased 40 percent over the 1946 models.

The new cab incorporated double-wall construction that gave greater strength and durability. Chevrolet ad writers described the Advance-Design cab as having "Unisteel Battleship" construction and "Observation Car Vision."

Cab-over-engine (COE) trucks were also all-new for 1947, being part of the two-ton 6000 series. The new cab-overs shared cab sheetmetal and most mechanicals with the conventional trucks. COEs were built on three wheelbases and in three configurations: cowl-chassis, cab-chassis, and complete trucks with one of eight stake or platform bodies. The most popular style was the short-wheelbase cab-chassis, which was used for tractor-trailer combinations. These trucks were among the most ruggedly handsome of any COEs ever built, yet accounted for only two percent of total production and are extremely rare.

One of two engines powered Advance-Design trucks. Thriftmasters used the 216-cid six, while Loadmasters got a 235-cid version. Forester green was the standard color; anything else was an extra-cost option.

No exterior changes occurred to the Chevrolet truck lineup for **1948,** though one new model was added. The addition was the model 3742, a forward-control delivery chassis with a 125¼-inch wheelbase. Buyers could choose from a number of body builders to supply delivery bodies in nine- or ten-foot lengths. The design allowed drivers easy access to the load area, and cut the turning circle by almost six feet. Prior to this, body manufacturers had to rework a conventional chassis at considerable expense to the customer.

On 3100 (½-ton) and 3600 (¾-ton) trucks, the shift lever was moved to the steering column and a foot-operated parking brake was used, thus allowing more foot room for a middle passenger. New to these trucks was an optional four-speed transmission to replace the standard three-speed.

Only minor refinements marked Chevrolet's **1949** trucks, the third year of the Advance-Design series. However, Sedan Deliveries adopted the styling of that year's all-new car line.

Beginning with the 1947 Advance-Design models, a plate attached to the sides of the hood contained the Chevrolet name and specified the size of the truck, either Thriftmaster or Loadmaster. The latter was thought to be too general, so for 1949, the series—3100, 3600, 3800, 4100 and so on—was carried on its own badge that sat below the Chevrolet nameplate. Also for '49, the gasoline tank was moved inside the cab and placed on the floor behind the seat. The gasoline filler cap was located on the right-hand side of the cab just behind the door handle.

Chevrolet's all-new 1949 car styling that graced the Sedan Delivery included a curved, two-piece windshield that emphasized the lower, wider design. Front fenders flowed smoothly into the bodysides, and rear fenders were just a sliver of their former, bulbous selves. Cargo capacity of the Sedan Delivery rose from 83 cu. ft. to 92.5, a considerable increase.

Partly due to the as-yet unsatiated pent-up postwar demand for vehicles and partly to the continued sales strength of its Advance-Design line and restyled Sedan Delivery, Chevrolet truck sales topped 345,000 for 1949—and would soon be going much higher.

1

2

1. A fixture in the Chevy truck line since 1928, the 1940 Sedan Delivery adopted the car line's new styling. This restored example has non-stock artillery-style wheels. **2.** Most 1940 Chevy trucks were little changed. This 1½-ton stake truck uses the conventional cab and a 133-inch-wheelbase chassis. **3.** Chevy trucks were restyled for 1941, and marketers placed the new face front and center in this advertisement. **4.** Selling points for the new 1941 trucks included power, economy, dependability, and driver comfort. The copywriters were also sure to point out that Chevy trucks were the best-selling trucks in the business.

1. America was out of the Depression by 1941, largely due to increased military production prompted by an alarming new war in Europe. Industry heeded President Roosevelt's call to become an arsenal of democracy. This eliminated unemployment, but brought on inflation. The 1941 Sedan Delivery again diverted from most other Chevy trucks by using the passenger car line's new styling. It also adopted a sturdier independent front suspension, a vacuum-assisted gearshift, and hydraulic shock absorbers.
2. Chevrolet's redesigned 1941 trucks also boasted in-fender sealed-beam "safety" headlamps. The standard engine was the same 90-horsepower six used in Chevy's cars. The ½-ton pickup remained the mainstay of the AK series.
3. The 1941 heavy-duty trucks also used the new styling. This dual-rear-wheel job was primarily meant for tractor-trailer duty.

1

2

3

The 1941 Chevrolet commercial lineup was the broadest in the company's history. There were two engines, three transmissions, five axle ratios, and nine wheelbases. This ½-ton pickup shows that the new design made for a streamlined workhorse. Driver comfort was addressed with features like a crank-open windshield and a comfortable seat that used a latex-bound hair pad on coil springs.

1

Chevrolet-built Pratt & Whitney engines power America's mightiest warplanes, including the C-82 Flying Boxcar, shown above.

CHEVROLET

America's Automotive Leader Gears All Its Resources to

"THE BIGGEST TRANSPORT JOB OF ALL TIME"

on land ... in the air ... all around the world

BUY MORE WAR BONDS
HELP SPEED THE VICTORY

Chevrolet has produced more than 475,000 military trucks in three different types, serving our fighting men everywhere.

CHEVROLET DIVISION OF GENERAL MOTORS

2

1. This advertisement was likely placed before Chevrolet ceased civilian production in late January 1942. **2.** As the war effort progressed, American companies, including Chevrolet, ran patriotically themed magazine ads that were intended to bolster home-front morale with the promise of speedy victory through mass production. **3.** During the war, the American military called on a wide array of manufacturers to provide trucks for the transport of troops and supplies. Chevrolet's specialty was the 1½-ton four-wheel drive G-7100 series. The 1942 Chevrolet G-7117 cargo truck shown here wears U.S. Navy colors.

After Allied victory in World War II, Chevrolet, like the rest of American industry, converted back to civilian production as quickly as possible. Chevrolet began production of "Interim" trucks on September 1, 1945. These were not considered 1946 model trucks, even though this line was made through April of that year. Chevrolet's official 1946 models did not enter production until May. These "postwar" models closely mirrored the 1941 models in level of equipment and marked the return of chrome trim. The ½-ton light-duty 3100 series included pickup, panel, canopy, and Suburban models. The 1946 Model 3106 Suburban was the priciest light-duty model, starting at $1283.

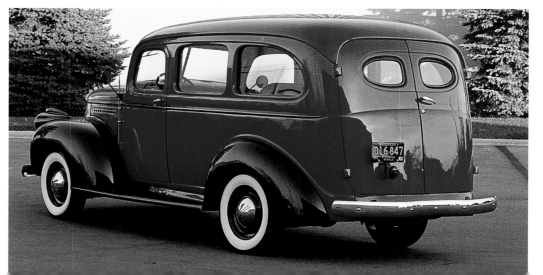

1

2

4

3

5

1. Like all of Chevrolet's ½-ton trucks, the Suburban was powered by a 216.5-cid inline six good for 90 horsepower. **2.** The Canopy Delivery combined features of the Panel Delivery and a pickup truck. **3.** As was common throughout the industry, Chevrolet's 1946 truck line was basically the same as the 1942 offerings. The ½-ton pickup started at $963. **4.** The painted grille suggests this pickup was one of the interim models produced in late 1945 and early 1946. After May 1, 1946, chrome grilles were once again standard on Chevy trucks. **5.** Postwar truckers found spartan, but efficient interiors.

Chevrolet continued making the 1941-style truck through the end of May 1947. These trucks were titled as 1946 or 1947 models, depending on when they were originally purchased. Chevrolet sold three basic series of light-duty trucks at this time. The ½-ton models were designated Series 3100, the ¾-ton models were Series 3600, and the one-ton units were Series 3800. This ¾-ton Delivery rode a 125¼-inch wheelbase, versus the 115-inch span the ½-ton model used. A one-ton delivery on a 134½-inch wheelbase was also available.

In mid 1947, Chevrolet, along with corporate cousin GMC, introduced restyled truck lines. These were the first rebodied General Motors postwar vehicles. The so-called "Advance-Design" trucks entered production in May, and officially went on sale on June 28, 1947. This ½-ton Deluxe Panel Delivery is a 1947 model.

A variation on the panel truck was the canopy express, which had large display areas cut into its sides and back. This 1948 ½-ton canopy express was joined by a larger one-ton version. Chevy's 1948 trucks were nearly identical to the '47s. Since the Advance-Design trucks were selling briskly in postwar America, there was little incentive, or need, for change.

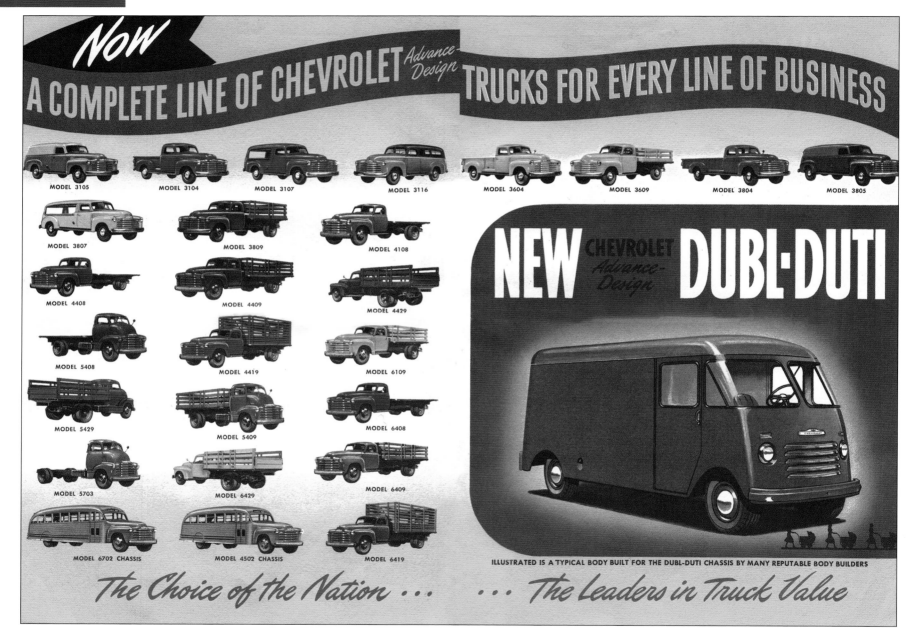

Now
A COMPLETE LINE OF CHEVROLET *Advance-Design* TRUCKS FOR EVERY LINE OF BUSINESS

MODEL 3105 MODEL 3104 MODEL 3107 MODEL 3116 MODEL 3604 MODEL 3609 MODEL 3804 MODEL 3805

MODEL 3807 MODEL 3809 MODEL 4108

MODEL 4408 MODEL 4409 MODEL 4429

MODEL 5408 MODEL 4419 MODEL 6109

MODEL 5429 MODEL 5409 MODEL 6408

MODEL 5703 MODEL 6429 MODEL 6409

MODEL 6702 CHASSIS MODEL 4502 CHASSIS MODEL 6419

NEW CHEVROLET *Advance-Design* DUBL-DUTI

ILLUSTRATED IS A TYPICAL BODY BUILT FOR THE DUBL-DUTI CHASSIS BY MANY REPUTABLE BODY BUILDERS

The Choice of the Nation ... ... The Leaders in Truck Value

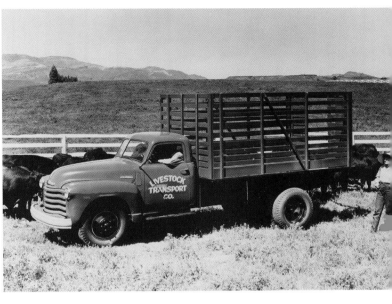

A 1948 brochure touted the complete line of Chevrolet Advance-Design trucks, that according to the company were "The Choice of the Nation" and "The Leaders in Truck Value." The new Dubl-Duti forward-control chassis was said to be suited to 9- or 10-foot custom-built panel bodies that could provide double the cubic load space of a conventional panel truck. Chevy offered light-duty Thriftmaster, heavy-duty Loadmaster, and cab-over-engine models. A wide variety of pickups, panels, chassis-cabs, school-bus chassis, and stake trucks were offered. Stake trucks were available in 17 models with payload capacities ranging from 1900 to 10,500 pounds. Promotional materials touted the Advance-Design trucks' combination of power and thrift. Chevy adwriters said the division's new trucks provided the three essentials for successful operation: Low first cost, low operating cost, and low maintenance cost.

Chevrolet trucks for 1949 looked the same, but a series of engineering improvements made the them stronger and more solidly built. Changes included the way the cab was mounted to the frame, additional bracing for the radiator support and hood, and a brighter taillight. Also, each truck's series was now identified by four-digit chrome numbers on both sides of the hood. Trucks in the 3100 to 4000 series used the 216.5-cid 90-bhp Thriftmaster Six. The 5000 and 6000 series received a standard 235-cid Loadmaster six, which offered little improvement in horsepower but usefully more torque. Chevy offered the bigger six as an option on the 4000 series trucks like this 1949 model 4400 tow truck (opposite page). The wrecker rides a 161-inch wheelbase and carries the standard four-speed manual transmission. This truck was originally owned by a Pennsylvania Chevrolet dealer, and is fitted with a Holmes 515E wrecker body.

CHAPTER 4
1950-1959

Despite receiving relatively few changes, Chevrolet pickups sailed through the Advance-Design era comfortably ensconced in first place in unit sales over arch-rival Ford.

The **1950** model year marked the fourth for the Advance-Design truck line, and alterations were minimal. The two-tone paint schemes that had been standard for Suburbans were dropped except for fleet use, but added were available panel-type rear doors that could be substituted for the traditional tailgate/liftgate arrangement. The new swing-out rear doors were easier to open when the driver had an arm full of packages, and if the Suburban was fitted with special bus equipment, passengers could now exit through the rear door.

Although the Thriftmaster's 216-cubic-inch engine showed a two-horsepower gain for 1950—from 90 to 92—the increase actually resulted from changes that occurred over a period of years since the last certified performance tests were run in 1941. Not to be outdone, the Loadmaster's 235-cid six also got a power boost, from 93 to 105 horsepower. The only notable chassis change occurred in the Thriftmaster series, as lever-action shocks gave way to double-acting airplane-style shocks. This change had been made on the car line—including the Sedan Delivery—in 1949.

For **1951,** Chevrolet's Advance-Design trucks received a number of minor alterations. The Sedan Delivery adopted the revised front end of the passenger-car line. Changes to the trucks included vent panes in the doors and elimination of the left-side cowl ventilator. A spotlight was newly optional. Safety was improved with new brakes on both the front and rear of series 3100 light-duty trucks and the Sedan Delivery. The reworked brakes provided smoother, more powerful braking action with less driver effort.

A new grille guard of a better design was made available for the 3100 and 3600 series. The new guard was lower, wider, and stronger. On heavy-duty conventional trucks, a chrome-plated grille was added as an option.

The rear bumper that had been standard equipment on ½- and ¾-ton chassis models and pickups now became an extra-cost option. With the rear bumper eliminated on 3100 and 3600 pickups, the tail lamp, license plate, tail pipe, and tire carrier were relocated or reworked so that they would

not project beyond the body where they might be damaged without the protection of the bumper. Without the rear bumper, the tailgate could be opened farther to hang straight down to ease loading.

Auxiliary stand-drive controls for the Forward Control chassis models were made extra cost items for 1951. These controls had been available before, but customers had to purchase them from the aftermarket supplier; now they could get them directly from Chevrolet.

For the **1952** model year, only a few exterior changes were made. One was that the turn-handle-type exterior door handles were swapped for push-button type, which were thought to be more attractive and easier to operate. Added as an option was a keyed lock for the left-hand door; previously, only the right-hand (passenger's) door had a keyed lock. Another change was prompted by material shortages caused by the Korean War: the deletion of Deluxe equipment and series nameplates, something that actually started in mid-1951. For the same reason, chrome-plated grilles and the extra-equipment rear bumpers were also dropped. On light- and medium-duty trucks, gray paint replaced chrome plating on bumpers and hubcaps.

On the one-ton series, a foot-operated parking brake replaced the floor-mounted hand-operated lever. This was the same mechanism as used in the ½- and ¾-ton models.

By **1953,** the Advance-Design was seven years old, and to those trying to tell the model years apart, any small change is a potential identifier. In this case, the telltale sign of a '53 is a more contemporary-styled hood nameplate that replaced the old series-designation plate.

New colors also made a visible distinction for the 1953 Chevrolet trucks. The standard color became Juniper Green with Cream Medium striping, but buyers could choose from a range of colors at no extra cost, and tinted glass became optional

A side-mounted spare-tire carrier mounted on the left side of the pickup box was offered as an option for ½-, ¾-, and one-ton models. Placing the side mount on ½-ton versions necessitated dishing out a small portion of the rear fender to accommodate the tire.

The 1953 Sedan Delivery was totally restyled again along with Chevrolet cars. The new body drew its smooth appearance from a revised grille, one-piece bumpers, curved windshield, and new parking and taillights. Styling made the model look longer than it was, as overall length was cut by two inches. Inside, the driver's compartment received a new instrument panel, a larger steering wheel, and revised colors and fabrics. The vent pane was now controlled by a small crank instead of the friction-type mechanism used since 1951.

This was the first year that directional signals were made available as a factory-installed accessory. The change was made because more and more states were requiring them on all new vehicles.

Surprisingly, **1954**—the final full year of the Advance-Design series—was a year of major changes. Exterior styling alterations were most evident in the parking lights and one-piece curved windshield. The latter served to improve both visibility and appearance.

On light-duty models, the hubcaps were stamped with the bowtie trademark instead of the Chevrolet name. The bowtie was painted blue, which made it stand out in contrast to the cream-colored hubcaps.

Greater comfort and safety were major features of a new interior. Changes included a restyled instrument panel and instruments, windshield garnish molding, steering wheel and horn button, and new interior colors and trim. The seat cushion, backrest and door panel were brown, while the instrument panel, garnish moldings, headlining, and door panels were beige.

Chevrolet trucks had a landmark year in **1955.** The Sedan Delivery—now known as the "1500 Series"—was again based on the car line, which carried sensational styling that would later make these vehicles among the most collectible in automotive history.

Early 1955 commercial trucks—called the "First Series"—were virtual carryovers from '54, but the entire Chevrolet light-duty truck line was radically redesigned for 1955's "Second series." A completely new cab and front-end design combined for a striking new look, and surveys taken during the development program to determine buyer needs and preferences dictated several mechanical and interior changes. Together, they resulted in an ultramodern appearance with many advantages in driver convenience and comfort.

Chevrolet dubbed its redesigned 1955 trucks the "Task Force" line. Styling hallmarks included the truck industry's first wraparound windshield, what Chevrolet advertising called a "Sweep-Sight Windshield." This idea was first shown the year before on GM's innovative Buick LeSabre concept Motorama show car. Other interesting styling innovations included shrouded headlights in visored fenders, a classic eggcrate grille, running boards concealed behind the cab doors, and an optional wraparound "full view rear window."

New features for driver convenience and ease of operation included power steering, power brakes, overdrive for ½-ton models, key-turn starting, tubeless tires, a 12-volt electrical system, and an optional four-speed automatic transmission for Series 3000 pickups.

Chevrolet's 1955 truck line was comprised of 75 models on 15 wheelbases. There were three forward-control chassis in place of the former two, but canopy express models were discontinued.

Nineteen fifty-five also brought the truck line's first V-8 engine. The famous "small-block Chevy" initially displaced 265 cubic inches and produced 156 horsepower in low-compression form with a two-barrel carburetor, 162 with higher compression, and 180 with high compression and a four-barrel carburetor. In light-duty trucks, it was offered as an option to the returning 235-cid six, which produced from 123 to 136 horsepower.

A new chassis featured an I-beam front axle and leaf springs for all wheels. Transmission choices included a three-speed manual with or without overdrive, a Heavy-Duty three-speed manual, a four-speed manual, and a four-speed automatic. Newly optional for 1955 was a planetary-type two-speed heavy-duty rear axle designed and built by Chevrolet.

Also new for 1955 was the Model 3204 long-box half-ton pickup, which rode a 123¼-inch wheelbase and carried a 90-inch long (7.5-foot) by 50-inch-wide cargo box. The Model 3604 ¾-ton pickup had the same dimensions. The model 3804 one-ton pickup had a 135-inch wheelbase chassis and carried a 108¼-inch long (9 foot) by 50-inch-wide cargo box.

Chevrolet dropped a bombshell on the industry in 1955 with the introduction of its limited-production Model 3124 Cameo Carrier. Its cab and front sheetmetal were the same as on other late-1955 ½-ton pickups, but in place of the traditional Stepside bed was a stylish cargo bed with full-width straight-sided fiberglass fenders that were affixed to a normal-width (48-inch) box. Today this kind of "styleside" bed is almost universal, but it was a novelty in 1955. A fiberglass tailgate cover was mounted over the steel tailgate and hid the hinges and latches for a sleeker look. All Cameos were painted Bombay Ivory with red accents.

The forward-control line was expanded to three models on three different wheelbases. New for 1955 were models 1442 and 1542, the former on a 104-inch wheelbase and the latter on a 125-inch span. All forward-control models for 1955 were rated at ¾-ton or one-ton.

The Sedan Delivery predictably adopted the car line's new **1956** styling, and equally predictably, the commercial line received few changes after its extensive 1955 makeover. However, the '56s were identified with a wider, lower-mounted hood badge and front-fender badges that were moved to above the side crease. For pickups, the V-8 now came in a lone 155-hp version, but the Sedan Delivery could have up to 205 hp. Cameo pickups expanded their color choices from one (Bombay Ivory) to eight.

Somewhat more significant changes marked the **1957** pickups. A new grille design featured an elongated oval floating in the grille's center, and hoods gained a pair of windsplits, similar to those found on Chevrolet's restyled '57 car line—which again played host to the Sedan Delivery. A Low-Hub steering wheel had its hub depressed three inches below the plane of the rim for added driver safety and better viewing of the instruments. The 265-cid V-8 offered in pickups got a boost to 162 hp, while the Sedan Delivery could be had with an enlarged 283-cid V-8 offering up to a rousing 270 hp—which could make for very fast deliveries indeed.

Perhaps most significant, however, was the midyear introduction of Chevrolet's first factory-built 4WD pickups. Previously, buyers wanting 4WD had to have aftermarket conversion kits installed, but they could now get ½- and ¾-ton 4WD pickups right from Chevrolet.

Most cars adopted the newly legalized dual headlights for **1958** (a few had them in '57), and Chevrolet was no exception. That extended to trucks as well, and the lights, along with a new grille beneath them, marked their most visible change since the design was introduced in late-1955.

But it certainly wasn't the only change. All light-duty pickups adopted the Apache name for 1958, and buyers were offered a choice of two beds: the traditional Stepside bed and a new straight-sided Fleetside bed. The latter looked similar to the Cameo's bed, but it was made of steel, had missile-shaped convex bulges along each side, and the inside was full width rather than the narrow 48 inches of the Cameo's box. With the advent of the Fleetside, the Cameo faded away and didn't return for 1959.

Chevrolet's car line was redesigned for 1958, and, as usual, the Sedan Delivery followed suit. Wheelbase grew from 115 inches to 117.5, and a new 348-cubic-inch V-8 was offered.

Chevrolet answered Ford's Ranchero in **1959** with the first of its famous El Camino pickups, making it Chevrolet's first car-based pickup since 1941. Like the Sedan Delivery, the El Camino carried that year's new automotive styling that featured huge "batwing" tailfins, but had a six-foot open bed behind a "glassy" two-seat cab. Engine choices ranged up to a 335-hp 348-cid V-8.

Commercial light-duty pickups received a revised grille, hood badge, and fender badges, but few other changes. Newly optional was a Positraction rear axle.

Chevrolet trucks closed out the 1950s exactly where they'd begun: at first place in sales. The decade saw a good-looking pickup turn into a great-looking one, along with the addition of new models, including the stylish El Camino. All in all, it was a great time to be a fan of the blue bowtie.

For the first time since 1935, Chevy offered two engines rather than just one in light-duty models: the familiar 216.5-cid six that produced 92 bhp, and a newcomer, a 235.5-cid six adapted from an existing truck engine. The new engine was fitted with hydraulic valve lifters and fed by a one-barrel carburetor, either a Rochester or (less frequently) a Stromberg, and cranked out 105 horsepower. The 1950 Special Sedan Delivery was one beneficiary. Sedan Delivery production for the model year topped 23,000, a record for the body style. The Sedan Delivery was popular with small businesses, as it could handle loads as lengthy as 73 inches; total load space was 92.5 cubic feet. Whitewall tires, which brought a touch of elegance, were extra-cost options. Note the slab-sided front fenders and side-hinged cargo door.

1

1. Where Sedan Delivery styling looked to the future, the '50 Suburban still carried cues from the Forties, notably bulging front fenders and a heavy grille dominated by five horizontal chromed strakes. Plainly not sleek, the Suburban was tidy and utilitarian, and though it could carry up to eight passengers, access to the second- and third-row seats wasn't easy in the truck's two-door form.
2. Suburban was well-liked by businesses, as this May 1950 magazine ad suggests. Optional chrome trim was late-Art Deco. 3. A 1950 pickup in Deluxe five-window form shows off its airy cab. The rear quarter windows weren't standard fare.

2

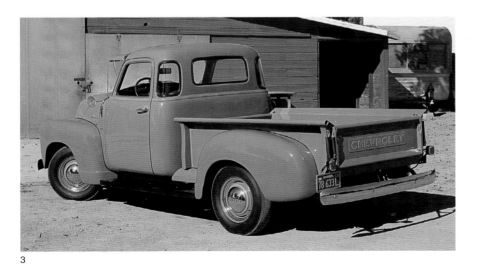

3

1

If it takes more power . . . and top payloads
IT'S A CHEVROLET JOB!

Big job? That's one for Chevrolet trucks with Loadmaster 105-h.p. engine. They're loaded with power—*greater net horsepower than any of the five most popular standard equipped makes in their weight class*, 13,000 to 16,000 lbs. G.V.W.* And here's the payoff on payloads, too. Chevrolet's economy of operation and upkeep, and rock-solid construction let you deliver the goods at *low cost per ton mile*. But that isn't all! In every other way, Chevrolet is a leader. When you see these trucks you'll know it for fact. You'll know why they outsell every other make, year after year! See your Chevrolet dealer. **Gross Vehicle Weight.*

CHEVROLET
ADVANCE-DESIGN TRUCKS

1. Advance-Design, by now in its fifth model year, continued to reap sales dividends for Chevrolet trucks in 1951. Advance-Design pickups, like the model 3100 shown here, had honest three-across seating and a cargo bed with a forward bias for better cargo management. **2.** Ads targeting buyers in construction and other trades emphasized the hardiness of the 105-bhp "Loadmaster," which brought "greater net horsepower than any of the five most popular standard equipped makes in their weight class . . . ." A 4-speed manual floor shift was mandatory at this weight class, and two-speed rear axles were available.

Changes to Chevrolet's 1952 truck line were modest, but as the Korean War ground on into 1951, one casualty for '52 was chrome, a material with wartime applications. Chevrolet trucks now had less visual sparkle than the year before. The change was most noticeable on the grillework, which looks sober and workman-like on this two-tone '52 pickup. Note the side-mounted spare tire and sun shields for the side glass. Lever-style door handles were replaced by a push-button design this year, and visibility while backing up was improved by a greater curve in the cab's quarter windows. Engines continued as before. The base pickup cost $1407 and had a load capacity of 1680 pounds.

2

3

CHEVROLET *Advance-Design* TRUCKS

NEW

POWER ★ PERFORMANCE ★ SAFETY ★ DURABILITY ★ ECONOMY

1

1. This Chevrolet truck brochure for 1953 emphasizes an array of new available colors and suggests the suitability of trucks for everyday suburban use. **2.** The $1947 116-inch-wheelbase 3100 Series pickup came standard with the 92-horsepower "Thriftmaster" six. **3.** Suburban offered traditional panel doors at the rear or the liftgate/tailgate arrangement shown. **4.** The ¾-ton pickup was called the 3600 Series for '53. Built-in stake pockets allowed for a canopy. **5.** The 3800 Series one-ton pickup had a 2900-pound payload capacity. **6.** Another 3800 Series, this one a dual-rear-wheel model toiling as a stake-bed truck. **7.** Even a full load of cake rolls probably didn't come close to taxing the payload capacity of this Forward Control truck. **8.** Six wheels were standard on the Model 6103 heavy hauler, which was capable of pulling up to 16,000 pounds. **9.** The Model 5703 Cab-Over-Engine featured pug-nose styling. **10.** Many a student was ferried to and from school on Chevrolet's Model 6802 School Bus Chassis.

4

5

8

6

9

7

10

1

2

4

3

1-2. The split windshield went away for 1954, and gauges were redesigned, as on this 3100 Series pickup. **3.** The hefty 3800 Series rode a 137-inch wheelbase and could be fitted with a variety of cargo beds. **4.** Buyers of 3100s might add the available spotlight, side-mounted spare, sun visor, and DeLuxe hood ornament. Chrome (on a new, split grille) was back. **5.** Advance-Design was still hyped in this truck-family ad from January 1955. **6-7.** For model-year 1955, Series 3100 Panels with Advance-Design cues were available for just three months; running boards and rounded fenders thus had their last hurrahs.

You won't find all these hour-saving, dollar-saving
'55 CHEVROLET TRUCK FEATURES *anywhere else!*

**Dollar-Saving
Engine Features**

You get exactly the right power for your job. All three great valve-in-head engines deliver gas-saving, hour-saving high-compression performance. Aluminum alloy pistons, all-weather ignition system, full-pressure lubrication, assure long low-cost life!

Trip-Saving Body Features

Chevrolet-built, Unit-Designed truck bodies last longer, require less maintenance. What's more, you haul big loads, save time and extra trips. New stake and platform bodies are wide, long

and roomy. Spacious pickups have sturdy tailgates that close grain-tight!

Long-Life Chassis Features

Sturdy single-unit tubular steel rear axle housings! Strong and rigid frames! Durable Diaphragm Spring Clutches with high torque capacities and long-life construction. Spring capacity is matched to tire capacity for dependable performance.

**Advance-Design
Cab Features**

Assured driver comfort with efficient ventilation and insu-

lation; shackle mountings that cushion frame vibrations; a one-piece curved windshield with full-width defroster outlet. The all-steel Double-Wall cab construction means extra safety and durability.

**Work-Saving
Control Features**

Less effort needed with Recirculating-Ball Steering Gear; Torque-Action and Twin-Action brake design helps you stop more surely and easily. Proved truck Hydra-Matic Transmission, optional on ½-, ¾- and 1-ton models at extra cost, eliminates clutching and gearshifting.

Take a good look at these '55 Chevrolet truck features, if you will. See how they'll save hours and dollars and driving effort on your hauling job. Then consider this: You won't find all these worthwhile advances in any other truck at any price. It's a fact! Chevrolet trucks bring you the features you want for '55 . . . the savings you want for years to come! See your Chevrolet dealer. . . . Chevrolet Division of General Motors, Detroit 2, Michigan

FIRST IN SALES *year after year!*

CHEVROLET ADVANCE-DESIGN TRUCKS

5

6

7

1

1. The 1955 truck line (now available with Chevy's new 265-cid V-8) flaunted startlingly new sheetmetal. The design included integrated front fenders, a dramatically wrapped windshield, hooded headlamps, and oblong grille—variations of what were used on Chevy's restyled 1955 cars. The changes were most dramatic on the Cameo Carrier ½-ton pickup, which featured a fiberglass-fendered straight-sided cargo bed in place of the normal Stepside steel bed. When new, the Cameo's high price made it a slow seller, but over time, it became a much-revered collectible.
2. Another '55 Cameo, in rear view, shows the full-body cargo bed that was made possible by the slab-sided fiberglass fenders. Bombay Ivory with red accents was the only color combination offered. **3.** Inside, the Cameo was distinctly carlike, with spiffy upholstery and a modern dash dominated by a hooded, triangular recess that contained the speedometer.

2

3

1. The 1955 "Task-Force" platform and stake truck catalog emphasized the line's versatility—and good looks. Left to right, the cover features a 1½-ton platform, ¾-ton stake, standard two-ton stake (in red), and two-ton short-wheelbase "Low Cab Forward" (LFC) stake. **2-3.** The ¾-ton stake had a usable bed width of 73 inches. **4-5.** The one-ton stake duallie had a wider bed of 85 inches. **6 (foreground)-7.** LCF models had a shorter nose and a high-mounted body that eliminated the floor tunnel hump. Their shorter wheelbase aided maneuverability. **8-9.** Maximum GVW of the 1½-ton Platform was 14,000 pounds. **10-11.** The 123-hp New Loadmaster six was standard on the two-ton stake; a 140-hp New Jobmaster variant was optional.

Modern Design for Modern Hauling
ALL-NEW CHEVROLET *Task-Force* **PLATFORM** AND **STAKE TRUCKS**

1

2

4

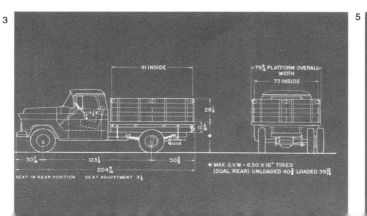

3

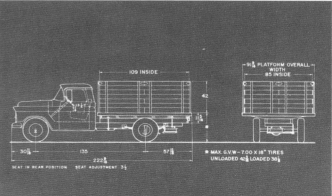

5

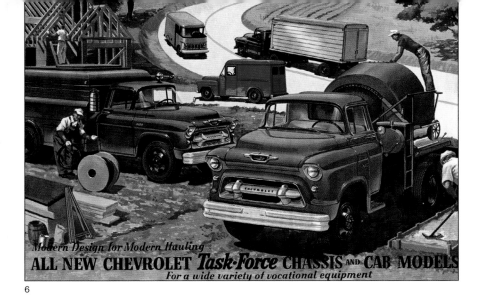

Modern Design for Modern Hauling
ALL NEW CHEVROLET *Task-Force* **CHASSIS** AND **CAB MODELS**
For a wide variety of vocational equipment

6

7

8

Low Cab Forward Model 5408 136½" Wheelbase
Here is a rugged, versatile stake body mounted on Chevrolet's revolutionary new Low-Cab-Forward truck chassis. Floor tunnel hump has been elimina

10

9

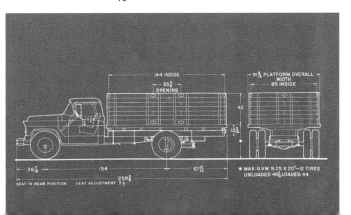

11

This '56 ½-ton pickup is powered by the 265-cid V-8 that had been introduced by Chevy for 1955. Called "Trademaster" for truck applications, the engine produced 155 hp. As small trucks became increasingly "personal," Chevy creature comforts and accessories were emphasized—such as the whitewalls and full wheel covers seen here. The hood emblem was new for '56, and the side nameplate was shifted to a location above the fender crease. Cabins were functional but hardly less comfortable than what a driver would find in a Chevy car. Although Chevy's uplevel Cameo had a slab-sided cargo bed, the ½-ton carried on with the venerable (and very practical) Stepside design, which would find renewed popularity—as a style statement—four decades later.

For 1957, the Cameo continued to excite buyers who wanted utility plus style, but a hefty price premium over a standard pickup kept sales low; a standard pickup started at $1800, while the Cameo cost $2273—and that was before adding some of its flashy options and a V-8 engine. This '57, in Bombay Ivory and Cardinal Red, is equipped with the optional V-8. Cameo production for the year was 2224 out of total pickup production of more than 198,000.

1

2

3

1. For 1957, Chevy trucks adopted a floating trapezoid grille as on this ½-ton pickup. **2.** Base-model ½-tons came standard with painted grille, bumpers, and headlamp surrounds instead of brightwork, but this pristine example is fitted with optional chrome bumpers and, on the inside, a radio. The ½-ton pickup weighed just over 3200 pounds and offered a payoad capacity approaching 1800 pounds. **3.** Some of Chevy's automotive styling touches for '57 carried over to the commercial trucks as evidenced by the twin wind split ornaments on the hood of this Suburban Carryall. Owners climbed into the cab via concealed "Safety Steps." This Suburban has panel doors at the rear; a wagon-type tailgate was also available.

1

2

3

4

5

6

1-3. Chevy's light trucks adopted dual headlights and the "Apache" name for 1958. **4-5.** The slow-selling Cameo returned for the '58 model year, but February 1958 brought a newly available "Fleetside" cargo-bed design to Chevy ½-tons. Because the new full-width steel-bed Fleetside looked much like the Cameo and cost just $1900 vs. Cameo's $2231, this new model soon rendered the Cameo an endangered species, making these two '58 Cameos among the rarest of the rare. **6.** The heavy-duty Series 80 came standard with dual 15,000-pound-capacity rear axles.

2

1

3

4

5

6

1. The least-expensive Apache pickup in the 1959 Cherolet line remained the ½-ton Stepside at $1948. **2-3.** This '59 Fleetside, base priced at $1964, shows off its round taillights and new two-tone paint scheme. **4.** The heavy-duty truck engines for '59 (from left): Jobmaster six, a pair of Taskmaster V-8s, Workmaster V-8, and Workmaster V-8 Special. **5.** Chevy countered Ford's Ranchero in 1959 with the graceful El Camino, which shared its "bat wing" styling with the car line. Its six-foot-long bed could carry up to 1150 pounds. **6.** The Sedan Delivery likewise took on the car line's look. **7.** The '59 Series 60 6303H had a GVW of 32,000 pounds.

7

Chevrolet's commercial pickups were redesigned for 1960 with rather odd, boxy styling topping a new chassis.

In 1959, Chevrolet's cars were given flat hoods that were flush with the tops and forward edges of the front fenders, eliminating the final vestiges of the "catwalk" that had always separated them. This theme carried into the commercial pickups for **1960,** as did the cars' "nostrils" above the headlights, though in exaggerated form. The trucks' grille, flanked by dual headlights on each side, rode in a band just above the bumper. The look was certainly more modern, if perhaps a bit strange to some eyes.

Less controversial were the chassis refinements. A solid front axle was replaced by an independent front suspension with torsion bars on all but the 4-wheel-drive models, which continued with the former setup. In back, ½- and ¾-ton pickups featured a two-link coil-spring rear suspension, while variable-rate leaf springs were standard for heavier-duty trucks.

Cabs now featured a new floor design that eliminated the concealed inner step. This resulted in more usable inside width—5.1 inches more shoulder room, 5.8 inches more hip room—and easier entry and exit.

Suburbans featured a new tailgate/liftgate design that permitted the liftgate to be raised independently of the tailgate, which allowed easier loading of small packages.

Added for 1960 was a line of low tilt-cab medium-duty trucks. Their compact dimensions and set-back front axle made these maneuverable workhorses well-suited to the urban delivery market.

For 1960, the engine lineup included four basic powerplants: the 235- and 261-cid sixes, and the 283- and 348-cid V-8s. The 235-cid Thriftmaster six was standard for all ½-, ¾-, 1½-, and light-duty two-ton models, except the ¾- and one-ton forward-control trucks, which used the Thriftmaster Special (with updraft carburetor). Heavy-duty two-ton trucks were standard with the 261-cid Jobmaster six. The 348-cid Workmaster Special was available on all lighter 2½-ton trucks except tandem-axle models; tandems and heavy 2½-ton trucks were powered by the rugged Workmaster 348-cid V-8. For the first time the optional 283-cid Trademaster V-8 engine was made available for the 4WD series. Still, Chevrolet sold seven six-cylinder-powered trucks for every one V-8 truck.

Returning for 1960 were the car-based El Camino pickup and Sedan Delivery, both adopting the slightly less exaggerated styling of that year's automotive line. It would be their final year in this form, however; the El Camino would soon return in a reduced size, and the Sedan Delivery would make a brief appearance much later in even smaller guise.

After their 1960 redesign, Chevrolet's commercial trucks changed little for **1961.** Half- and ¾-ton pickups retained their Apache 10 and Apache 20 badges, respectively, but front-end styling was revised. Both offered an eight-foot cargo box, though a 6½-foot box was standard on ½-tons; either size could be had in Stepside or Fleetside form. Alternators (to replace a generator) were offered for the first time.

New to the lineup were a trio of light-duty haulers based on the rear-engine Corvair passenger car introduced for 1960. All were flat-front forward-control models that fell under the R1200 or "Corvair 95" series. Included were the Model R1205 Corvan, a panel-delivery vehicle; the Model R1244 Loadside pickup; and the Model R1254 Rampside pickup, which had a fold-down side loading ramp.

All Corvair 95 models were built on a 95-inch wheelbase with a nominal ½-ton payload rating. All featured body-frame integral construction; four-wheel coil-spring independent suspension; a rear-mounted, horizontally-opposed, six-cylinder air-cooled engine; and a choice of 3-speed manual, four-speed manual, or Powerglide automatic transaxle.

Chevrolet's truck lineup expanded to 203 different models for **1962,** the largest in its history. Conventional pickups featured front-end styling revisions that did away with the huge oval-shaped hood nostrils, and single headlights replaced the former dual units. The Apache name was dropped, so badges read, for instance, "C10" on a 2-wheel-drive ½-ton short bed, "K20" on a 4-wheel-drive ¾-ton short bed. The long-bed (eight-foot) versions of those trucks would be C15 and K25.

Other notable changes occurred in the powertrain lineup. Four new engines were offered, including two V-8 gas units of 327 and 409 cubic inches, and two diesel engines of four- and six-cylinder design. Discontinued were the 283-cid Taskmaster V-8 and the 348-cid Workmaster Special, which was a distinct version of the regular 348 Workmaster.

Perhaps the most notable changes for **1963** involved job-tailored chassis, which provided specific designs to better fit the requirements of each nominal weight rating. Ladder-type frames of thicker metal were used for all conventional-line models for greater durability. Front coil springs replaced torsion bars on all pickups, and on ½- and ¾-ton versions, two-stage coil rear springs and optional cantilever leaf-type auxiliary springs increased payload capacity.

Meanwhile, a new 230-cid six-cylinder engine replaced the 235-cid unit during the year, and a new 292-cid six replaced the old 261. The latter two changes were particularly significant because about 80 percent of Chevrolet trucks during this period were fitted with six-cylinder engines. All engines for 1963 were equipped with closed crankcase ventilation systems.

Although several changes marked Chevrolet's **1964** truck lineup, perhaps the biggest news was the return of the El Camino after a three-year absence. It was again based on a passenger car, but this time it was Chevy's new midsize 115-inch-wheelbase Chevelle; previously, it was based on the 119-inch-wheelbase full-size line. It featured a 6½-foot cargo bed that was 46 inches wide between the wheelwell hous-ings. Engine choices ranged up to a 250-hp 327-cid V-8.

Nearly as notable was the addition of the front-engine/rear-drive G10 panel van. Though it rode a five-inch-shorter wheelbase than its Corvair-based Corvan sibling, it was about the same size overall. But whereas the Corvan had a hump at the rear of the cargo floor to clear its rear-mounted engine, the G10 had a floor that was flat nearly all the way to the front seats. Its engine was mid-mounted—just behind the front axle—and protruded a bit into the load area, but this arrangement was preferable for many uses. The standard engine was a 90-hp 153-cid four, but a new 120-hp 194-cid six—which was standard in the El Camino—was optional. With a starting price of $2067, the G10 cost $145 less than a Corvan with its 95-hp flat six (110-hp optional), and would soon replace it.

On conventional pickups, the biggest change was in the cab. Previously, a wraparound windshield resulted in forward-slanted front roof pillars, but a new flatter windshield brought rear-slanted front roof pillars. It also necessitated revised doors, side windows, and vent panes.

The rear-engine Corvan was dropped for **1965,** and most Chevrolet trucks saw only minor styling changes. However, air conditioning became a factory option, and the El Camino could now be ordered with a more potent 350-hp version of the 327 V-8, or with a new 375-hp 396-cid "big block" V-8. Chevrolet truck production topped 600,000 units for 1965—a new record.

A redesigned Chevelle passenger car resulted in a new

look for the **1966** El Camino—at least for the front half. The cargo bed was carried over, but new fenders and grille provided a more "chiseled" look to the stylish pickup.

The G-Series Chevy Van lost its previously standard four-cylinder engine, leaving the 194-cid six as the base engine, with a 230-cid six optional.

After a record-setting '65, Chevrolet's commercial trucks saw few changes for 1966. However, pickups were newly available with a 250-cid six or a 327-cid V-8. The latter was offered alongside the 283 V-8 and was rated at the same 220 hp as the top version of the smaller engine, but it produced more torque.

A complete redesign of Chevrolet's commercial trucks for **1967** resulted in what were sometimes called the "Glamour Pickups." Gone were the somewhat over-styled lines of the previous version, replaced by a clean, chiseled appearance. Interiors were new, too, and could be dressed up to carlike levels. It was during this generation that pickups made a major transition from being merely utilitarian to high-styled "personalized" vehicles. The pickup-based Suburban got the same treatment. Oddly, both it and the panel version were sold in a three-door body style, with one door on the driver's side and two on the passenger's side.

Although Chevrolet still sold slightly more sixes than V8s, for the first time, the opposite was now true for the industry in general—and Chevrolet would join the trend in '68. Part of this was due to America's newfound love affair with the RV. Recreational Vehicle sales were kicking into high gear, and pickups were often the vehicle of choice to either pull them or carry them; travel trailers, hi-low trailers, and slide-in campers were becoming ever more popular. Because RVing was enjoyed by the whole family, there was a great amount of interest in pickups with style, power, automatic transmissions, power assists, air conditioning, and comfortable cab interiors, and Chevrolet responded to the demand.

The new 1967 Chevrolet pickups were referred to as "A new concept in personalized pickups." The sleek lines were accompanied by a new lower height for easier entry, more-comfortable cab interiors, new power, an upscale Custom Sport Truck (CST) model that featured the comfort and appearance of a passenger car, and an all-new 4WD system.

Front suspensions for all Chevrolet trucks continued to be independent with coil springs. For Series 10 and 20 pickups, coil spring rear suspensions were also standard equipment. Leaf springs were standard for Series 30 trucks. Auxiliary rear springs were offered for Series 10 and 20 trucks.

Chevrolet's camper pickup line was enhanced for 1967 by the addition of the CST luxury cab interior package and Custom Camper packages for Series 10, 20, and 30 models. Custom Camper equipment included front stabilizer bars and heavier springs, shocks, wheels, and tires for better load-handling characteristics. Also new were hazard warning lights, an energy-absorbing steering column, and a padded dashboard

Chevrolet's light-duty engine lineup for 1967 consisted of

the 250- and 292-cid sixes, the 283-cid V-8, and the 220-hp 327 V-8. Four-wheel-drive pickups had a lower look due to redesigned powertrain components that reduced the overall height of the truck by five inches while still retaining a transfer-case-to-ground height of 12½ inches. This was done by relocating the transfer case to a higher position and by attaching it directly to the transmission.

Although the commercial pickups certainly received top billing, there were other changes as well for 1967. The El Camino got a restyled cargo box and new tail treatment with wraparound taillights. Also new was a restyled G10 Chevy Van. It was still offered in short- (90 inch) and long- (108 inch) wheelbase versions. Headlights that had formerly been mounted high, just below the lower edge of the windshield, were dropped down and resided within an oval grille just above the front bumper.

The **1968** commercial pickups carried over with only minor visual changes, the most noticeable being the addition of federally mandated side marker lights. Engine choices were shuffled as a 307-cid V-8 replaced the 283, and a new 310-hp 396 was added to the options list.

More significant was a redesigned El Camino. It again followed the styling lead of the Chevelle—at least in front—but added "flying buttress" rear roof pillars that gave it a racy look. That could be amplified by ordering the new SS 396 (Super Sport) package, which included special wheels and trim along with a 325-hp 396-cid V-8; 350- and 375-hp versions were optional.

Also in 1968, Chevrolet marked its 50th anniversary as a truck manufacturer, and celebrated by setting a new sales record at more than 800,000 units.

Commercial pickups got a blockier hood and revised grille for **1969** that gave them a noticeably different look, but they weren't the big news of that year's lineup. Nor was the El Camino, which got a fresh face of its own.

No, the biggest headlines were reserved for a new variant of the pickup called the Blazer. Latching onto a trend started by the Jeep CJ and picked up in the mid-'60s by the Ford Bronco, the Blazer was Chevrolet's first attempt at what is today known as a sport-utility vehicle, or "SUV." And quite a successful attempt it was.

The Blazer rode a shortened pickup chassis and carried pickup sheetmetal, but had a rear seat along with a roof that could be completely removed. It was initially offered only in 4WD form, as were the Jeeps and Broncos against which it competed as an "off road" vehicle.

New to Chevrolet's engine roster was a 350-cid V-8 that replaced the 327. Like its predecessor, it slotted between the 307 V-8 and the big-block 396s, and offered from 255 to 350 hp; the 396 offered as much as 375 hp.

One more change marked the 1969 Chevy truck lineup, and it was a big one—literally. For the first time, Chevrolet nameplates graced heavy-duty over-the-road trucks that had formerly been exclusive to sister-division GMC. With that, Chevrolet closed out the 1960s as a full-line truck manufacturer, and would expand that even further in the '70s.

1. Chevy's 1960 trucks were fully redesigned. Cabs were lower, roomier, more durable, and arguably more contemporary in appearance, even though the double nostrils above the grille looked like a throwback to the company's 1959 passenger car styling. Chevy's light-duty trucks also featured a new chassis. In the front, there was an independent torsion-bar suspension. Out back, the solid rear axle was located by two trailing arms and a lateral stabilizer bar, and suspended by two coil springs. 2. The new cab was up to seven inches lower, yet the company said it offered more hip, leg, and head room than the 1959 Chevrolet cab. The new instrument panel placed all gauges and controls directly in front of the driver, and the seat was five-inches wider than before. 3. Chevy Stepside pickups used a bed with a wood floor and a grain-tight tailgate. Running boards between the cab and rear fenders assisted side loading. The Apache 10 Stepside was available in short- and long-wheelbase models. The long-wheelbase truck shown here rode a 127-inch span. 4. Chevy continued to offer chassis/cab models that could be fitted with job-specific bodies by outside vendors.

1

2

3

4

1

1. This illustration shows the height difference between the 1960 truck and a comparable 1959 model. **2-3.** The car-based El Camino and Sedan Delivery used that year's toned-down styling. El Camino production came in at 14,163 units, while a mere 3034 Sedan Deliverys were made. Both vehicles were in their final season as full-size models. **4-5.** Chevrolet also introduced a new line of Tilt Cab trucks for 1960. The short, cab-forward design offered advantages like more room for bodies and cargo, the ability to carry heavier loads, and city-friendly maneuverability.

4

2

3

5

1

2

3

4

5

6

7

1-4. Chevy added a line of compact Corvair-based trucks in 1961, which included cargo and window vans along with a pickup. The last was offered as a Loadside model that had a tailgate, and as a Rampside that added a fold-down side ramp.
5-8. The standard Apache pickups received only detail changes this year. Buyers were starting to appreciate the slicker looks and extra cargo volume of the Fleetside bed design, but the traditional Stepside model still found customers as well.

8

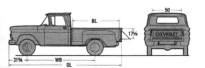

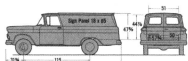

Chevrolet offered a dozen 4-wheel-drive models for 1961, including Fleetside and Stepside pickups, panel delivery, Suburban, and chassis cab models. The 4-wheel-drive system allowed the truck to be driven on the highway in 2-wheel drive, and shifted into 4-wheel mode when extra traction was needed. Chevy's tandam-axle heavy-duty trucks (top right) were driven by the two rear axles. These tough trucks were powered by the Workmaster 348-cid V-8 engine.

Chevrolet's wide-ranging truck line was juggled a bit for 1962, so it now encompassed 203 models. The light-duty pickups were no longer called Apaches. All conventional-cab models received a cleaner hood design that did away with the "nostrils" used the previous two years, and most switched to single, rather than dual, headlights. Gas engines were available in a variety of six- and eight-cylinder configurations that could suit most any job, and GM's two-cycle diesel power was available for medium- and heavy-duty models. Chevrolet had America's best-selling truck line in 1962.

Chevrolet called the 1962 Suburban Carryall a first-class example of functional styling and all-purpose utility. The truck-based wagon could seat eight passengers or carry up to 950 pounds of payload. The bench seats were covered in a combination of vinyl and cloth. The right-front seat folded forward for access to the back seats, or the rear seats could be removed to provide 155 cubic feet of cargo space. The sliding rear-side windows were optional, and buyers were offered the choice of station wagon or panel-type rear doors. There were three engines to choose from: a 235-cid inline six rated at 135 horsepower, a 261-cid six that was good for 150 horses, or a 283 V-8 that made 160. Three- and four-speed manual transmissions or Chevy's Powerglide automatic were available.

The Corvair 95 Rampside pickup soldiered on into 1963 largely unchanged. Most people who remember them have a fondness for these Corvair workhorses. Compared to contemporary Volkswagen trucks, they were larger and faster—and because of their superior heater, warmer in winter. In the end, the Corvair trucks were no more successful against Ford's Econoline than the Corvair had been against the Falcon. One by one they disappeared: the Loadside pickup in early 1962, Corvan and Rampside in 1964, and the Greenbrier passenger model in 1965.

For 1963, Chevy's light-duty trucks received a new grille, but otherwise their exterior appearance was little changed. There were improvements, but they were hidden under the skin. The company said the new frames were lighter but stronger, and the light-duty line benefited from a new independent front suspension that used coil springs instead of torsion bars. There were two new inline six-cylinder engines as well: a 230-cid unit with 140 bhp, and a 292 rated at 165 bhp.

1964 CHEVROLET TRUCKS

1

3

4

5

1-4. Don't let appearances fool you; Chevy's conventional truck cab was dramatically reworked for 1964. The changes centered around eliminating the wraparound portions of the windshield, and included new front pillars and door frames. Expected grille and trim changes were executed as well. **5.** Chevy's tilt-cab models received a new front suspension in 1963 that substituted leaf springs and a beam axle for the independent torsion bar set up used previously. This 1964 model shows off the line's new grille.

1

4

2

3

1-3. Chevy's El Camino resurfaced for 1964, but it was now based on the mid-size Chevelle. The 1965 model shown here sported a newly styled front end and revised trim. A base '65 El Camino started at $2270 with a 120-horse 194-cid six. **4-5.** The medium- and heavy-duty trucks were still available in a wide variety of configurations. The C Series (below) used a single rear axle, and the M Series (above) had tandem rear axles. These two lines were gas powered, with available engines ranging from the 292 six to a 409-cid V-8. GM's 6V-53 Diesel engine was available in the E, U, and W Series heavy-duties.

5

1-4. Chevy pickups continued to evolve through the 1960s with minor trim and equipment changes each year, plus the occasional new mechanical or convenience feature. This ½-ton 1965 Fleetside used the longer 127-inch wheelbase to accommodate an eight-foot cargo box. The 115-inch short chassis mounted a 6.5-foot bed. Not many folks bought pickups as an alternative to the car in 1965, and Chevy's truck cabs reflected that with a practical but spartan work-oriented cabin decor. The standard 230-cubic-inch inline six is found under this truck's Cardinal Red hood. The 140-horsepower engine mates to a three-speed manual transmission. So equipped, this Fleetside started at $2060: A Stepside model was $16 cheaper. Despite the few changes, Chevrolet truck production topped 600,000 units for 1965—a new record.

1

2

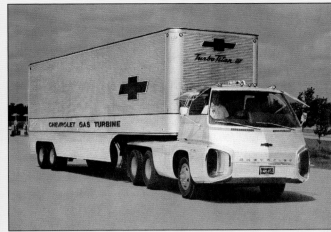

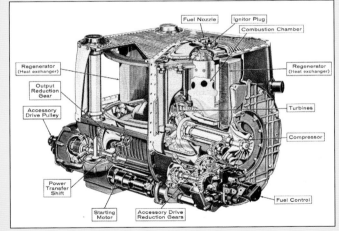

3

4

TURBO-TITAN III

The Turbo-Titan III was Chevy's third gas-turbine-powered dream truck. The so-called "Truck of Tomorrow" was based on a standard tilt-cab model with unique exterior styling and a luxurious leather-trimmed interior. The GT-309 gas turbine engine was said to be the truck engine of the future.

Again showing little evident year-to-year change was the 1966 edition of Chevrolet's workhorse C-10 Stepside pickup, here in short-box 115-inch wheelbase form. The most obvious visual difference was the new model badge on each front fender. There was news under the hood, since pickups were newly available with a 250-cid inline six and a 327-cid V-8. The latter was offered alongside the 283 V-8, and although the 220-horsepower rating was the same as the smaller engine, the 327 produced more torque. No matter the body color, the interior sheetmetal was painted medium fawn.

1

4

3

1-2. Long-bed ½-ton pickups continued to use an eight-foot box and a 127-inch wheelbase that was shared with Chevy's ¾-ton models. The basic 1960 design made its last appearance for 1966. **3.** Like the pickups on which it was based, Chevy's 1966 Carryall Suburban continued largely unchanged. Panel door versions sold a bit better than the tailgate style shown here. **4.** For 1966, the El Camino adopted the Chevelle's new styling. El Camino was the only light-duty 1966 Chevy truck available with the 396-cid "Big Block" V-8.

1

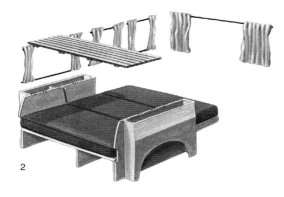

2

3

4

1-3. Chevy's compact G10 vans returned for 1966 with few changes. Panel and windowed Sportvan models remained available. The standard engine was now the 194-cid six rather than the 153-cid four. Chevrolet's extensive line of accessories included this sleeper unit that could help convert a Sportvan into a camper. **4.** New for 1966 were the high-tonnage 70000 and 80000 Series trucks available in tilt-cab and newly styled conventional models. These big rigs had GCW ratings up to 65,000 pounds. **5-6.** Other 1966 heavy-duty models used the same tilt-cab or existing pickup-based conventional cab as before.

5

6

New Chevy Sportvan leaves nothing to be desired (except trips to fascinating places)

There's a bigger size, a smoother ride, a flashy V8 ...and a low price tag!

CHEVROLET

a brand new breed for '67!

With extra room, extra power, the all-new Chevy Sportvan 108 is built for both people and their paraphernalia. There's space inside for everything for everyone—from the gun clubbers to the bubble gum clubbers. The body's 18 inches longer—you can tote the tall ones and the toddlers with room to spare.

Or you might prefer the Chevy Sportvan 90. This one has loads of room for 8 adults, or room to load 204 cubic feet of gear.

Whichever way you go, you can choose your degree of luxury. Pick from the regular Sportvan, Custom Sportvan or the Deluxe Sportvan—either size,

the long-wheelbase 108 or regular 90.

Both sizes float you along smoothly on new tapered-leaf springs. Both are available with either bigger 6-cylinder power for '67 or—for the first time—hustling V8 power.

And both offer picture window visibility all around, bucket-type driver and front-passenger seats standard, plus options and accessories for everything from a family picnic to a week in the wilderness. All this and a low price tag, too! Look in on your Chevy dealer and look in on a brand new breed of Sportvan for '67. . . . Chevrolet Division of General Motors, Detroit, Michigan.

1

2

1. Chevy's front-engine Sportvan was revised for 1967. The original 90-inch wheelbase was joined by a 108-inch version. Also new was a standard 230-cid inline six and an optional V-8. **2.** Chevy's Series 40, 50, and 60 conventional trucks wore new styling for '67. A wide variety of configurations and gas or diesel engines were available. **3.** The standard cab came with a 59½-inch-wide vinyl-trimmed bench seat, a driver's sunvisor, dome light, and a black rubber floor mat. **4.** Opting for the Custom comfort and appearance option added a foam-padded cloth and vinyl seat, armrests, and other niceties.

3

4

1. Chevrolet's pickup trucks were redesigned for 1967. Fleetside (shown) and Stepside models were still offered, and the new styling was also used on other light-duty models like the Panel Delivery and Suburban. In advertisements, Chevy bragged that the new pickup's looks were so striking, that if it looked any better, the company would have to stop calling it a truck. Talking points included color-keyed interiors, along with claims that the body offered better rust resistance and the bed was stronger. There was a new Custom Sport truck (CST) model that added standard bucket seats. **2-3.** The basic design carried over for 1968 with only minor changes to the trim and the addition of side-marker lights.

1

1-2. Chevy's car-based El Camino pickup was restyled for 1968. Still following the midsize Chevrolet Chevelle's design, the new El Camino rode a 116-inch wheelbase and had an overall length of 207 inches. The bed was able to carry objects more than six feet long and used double sidewall construction. There was additional storage space under the front portion of the bed that was accessible from behind the driver's seat. In keeping with the muscle-car craze sweeping the nation, El Camino could now be ordered with an SS 396 package (shown) that closely mirrored the content of the similar package for the Chevelle. The "big-block" 396-cubic-inch engine put out 325 horsepower in standard form with a 350-horse version optional. The handsome hauler's interior largely duplicated the front section of a comparably equipped Chevelle. Standard and optional Custom interiors included a bench seat, but the Custom interior could also be ordered with Strato-Bucket seats. **3.** For 1969, the El Camino was little changed. A new grille, revised side marker lights, a restyled dashboard, and shuffled trim were among the few items that helped keep the car-based hauler fresh.

3

Chevy added a new off-road vehicle for 1969, the K5 Blazer. Based on Chevy's light-duty truck, Blazer was an open-topped 4-wheel-drive vehicle that helped define what we now know as the sport-utility vehicle, or SUV. Based on a ladder-frame chassis, all Blazers had a heavy-duty suspension and 4-wheel drive. Blazers could be equipped to seat from one to five passengers; a single driver's seat was standard, while the second front seat and a rear three-person bench cost extra. Also available was a removable fiberglass roof. An inline six-cylinder engine was standard, but a variety of V-8s were available. The Blazer's front-end styling was the same as the revised look used on that year's other light-duty Chevy trucks. First-year Blazer production totaled 4935 units.

CHAPTER 6

1970-1979

After the halcyon days of the '50s and '60s, automakers faced some tough times in the '70s. New government regulations—particularly those governing exhaust emissions and fuel economy—presented huge challenges never before faced by Detroit. Overall, the decade is usually remembered as a dark time in the industry, but it was actually a rather positive period for trucks.

As the '70s dawned, the hurdles that lay ahead were not yet evident to the average buyer. Horsepower was in its heyday, styling was as good as ever, and all was right with the automotive world; the truck world, too, as sales remained strong.

For **1970,** Chevrolet's El Camino adopted a restyled front end with the "flatter" face that graced that year's Chevelle, the midsize car on which the El Camino was based. The standard engine was a 155-hp 250-cid six, but a host of V-8s were also offered. The potent, formerly top-line SS 396 model returned, but was joined by an even more potent SS 454 offering as much as 450 hp from its 454-cid V-8. Otherwise, the El Camino carried on with a

6.5-foot bed behind a two-door cab.

Few changes marked the conventional light-duty pickup line, which continued with a choice of short (6.5-foot) and long (eight-foot) beds in either Stepside or Fleetside form, and with either 2-wheel drive or 4-wheel drive. Engine choices ranged from a 250-cid six to a 310-hp 400-cid V-8. New options included AM/FM radio, stereo tape player, and tilt steering wheel. Also available were auxiliary fuel tanks on ¾- and one-ton units, and air-inflatable shocks on models with coil springs. Four-wheel-drive models were available with the three-speed Turbo Hydra-Matic automatic transmission. The truck-based Blazer SUV with its removable top that had been introduced for 1969 with 4WD now also came in a 2WD version.

The Chevy Van was likewise little changed, again offered in two lengths with either ½- or ¾-ton capacity. Engine choices were a 250-cid six or a 307-cid V-8.

Chevrolet ventured into the extra-heavy-duty market with the addition of new top-of-the-line Titan 90 Series tractors. These trucks were offered in several cab styles: two conventional trucks with BBC (bumper to back of cab) dimensions of 93 and 115 inches, plus a handsome 54-inch BBC aluminum tilt cab that was also offered in 74- and 86-inch BBC sleeper versions. The largest trucks ever offered by Chevrolet came in 22 basic models with GCW ratings up to 76,800 lb. Power options included Detroit Diesel and Cummins engines.

Some additions and revisions marked the **1971** Chevrolet truck lineup. Slotted in at the bottom was a Panel Express version of the new-for-1971 Vega, a four-cylinder subcompact car aimed at the growing number of fuel-efficient imports such as Volkswagens and Toyotas. The Panel Express was a two-door wagon with blanked-out side windows—essentially a tiny reincarnation of the former Sedan Delivery that disappeared in the early '60s. Power came from a 2.3-liter (140-cid) engine offering 90-110 hp.

Redesigned for 1971 was the Chevy Van. It now had a "nose" on what had been a completely flat face, giving it a much more modern look. The hood also provided outside access to the front of the engine for checking fluids. The truck offered a more comfortable ride than the previous model, as the driver was no longer sitting directly over the front axle. As before, it was offered in two lengths, but a one-ton version joined the ½- and ¾-ton models.

By contrast, Chevrolet's conventional pickups carried on with few changes. However, they became the first in their field to offer standard front disc brakes. The pickup-based Blazer SUV likewise was a virtual carryover.

As per tradition, the El Camino took the look of its automotive donor, the Chevelle, which for '71 adopted a single-headlight front end. It was also the truck most affected by that year's line-wide abandonment of high-compression engines, the result of a national phase-in of lower-octane low-lead gas. As a result, the top 454-cid V-8 was down from 450 hp to 425—hardly a crippling demotion.

In the medium-duty line, Chevrolet brought the Allison AT 540 automatic transmission to the 1971 models. Chevrolet was one of the first firms to offer it and made it available on

40, 50, and 60 Series single-axle trucks with V-8 engines. Other features of the 1971 medium-duty line were high-intensity headlamps and anti-theft door locks.

By the early '70s, a change was taking place among pickup buyers. No longer were they purchasing pickups solely for hauling lumber, ladders, or sacks of grain. In fact, some rarely hauled anything at all.

More and more, customers were buying pickups primarily for personal transportation, often to replace a second car in the family driveway. Chevrolet found this out the hard way in **1972** when demand for its pickups outstripped production capacity. All told, full-size pickup production hit nearly half-a-million units. By far the most popular model was the Fleetside C10 2-wheel-drive ½-ton, overwhelmingly in the long-bed version—possibly because its longer wheelbase made for a smoother ride. Not surprisingly, the same held true for the ¾-ton versions.

Commercial pickups saw few changes for 1972 except that engines suffered an apparent horsepower hit, though it was due more to a new rating system than to any actual loss in power. All engines now carried a "net" horsepower rating rather than the previous "gross" horsepower rating. They differ in that net horsepower is measured with the air cleaner, the exhaust system, and all accessories (such as alternators and power-steering pumps) in place and functioning. These all sap power, so the net rating was significantly lower than the old gross rating—which was sometimes included in advertising so the apparent loss in power was less shocking and somewhat explained. For example, a

350-cid V-8 offered in several trucks was rated at 250 gross horsepower, 175 net horsepower—a drop of about 30 percent.

The Chevy Van, El Camino, and Vega Panel Express likewise saw few changes other than a switch to net horsepower ratings, but added to the light-duty line was a compact pickup truck called the LUV—for Light Utility Vehicle. The LUV was built by Isuzu of Japan, carried a 111-cid (1.8 liter) 75-net-horsepower four-cylinder engine, and was rated at ½-ton capacity. However, it was much smaller than a conventional ½-ton short-bed pickup, as it had a 102.4-inch wheelbase (vs. 115) and weighed 2360 lb. (vs. about 3450 lb.). It also cost less: $2196 vs. $2680. Only about 21,000 LUVs were sold that first year (vs. nearly 62,000 C10 short-beds), but it gave Chevrolet a competitor to the small pickups from Nissan and Toyota.

Commercial pickups were redesigned for **1973** with a new chassis and fresh sheetmetal, and they gained a four-door crew-cab body style that could seat up to six. Styling was "squared up" and featured a wide, concave cove that went up the side of the front fender next to the headlight, then turned and ran straight back along the top edge of the body all the way to the rear of the truck (or cab in the case of a Stepside cargo bed). Low-mounted wraparound taillights were fitted in back and also served as the side marker lights. Wheelbases were longer thanks to the front axle being moved farther forward and the rear axle being moved farther back. Newly available was full-time 4-wheel drive. Engine power generally dropped somewhat across the board due to tighter emission standards, but added to the roster was a big-block 454-cid V-8 bringing a healthy 240 net horsepower, the same as the previous 402-cid (often still referred to as a "396") V-8 it replaced. In the cab, a new instrument panel was fitted, legroom was increased about 1½ inches, there was a new option that offered a stowage compartment behind the seat, and ventilation was improved. The Blazer and Suburban again mimicked the styling and engineering of the big pickups.

El Caminos were also redesigned for 1973, again following the lead of the Chevelle on which they were based. This included single round headlights in square pods flanking a rectangular grille with "wings" that extended below the headlights, all above the newly mandated five-mph front bumper, which was supposed to be able to take a five-mph hit without damage. Joining the returning SS package were the Estate, with two-tone paint scheme, and the Conquista, with wood-grain trim. Power choices ranged to the 240-horse 454-cubic-inch V-8.

Most of the news for **1974** wasn't about new vehicles or exciting engineering developments but about minor changes and refinements. Most notable of these was a new front end for the Vega Panel Express, which featured the slanted grille and larger bumpers shared with the cars. However, there was one new model: a Cutaway Van for use as a motor home chassis.

Aside from minor styling revisions, **1975** was largely a stand-pat year. However, new for 4WD pickups was an optional 400-cid V-8 between the 350- and 454-cid engines.

In response to tightening emissions regulations, all Chevrolet trucks up to 6000 lb. GVW (Gross Vehicle Weight) were, for the first time, equipped with a catalytic converter. They required the use of lead-free gas along with periodic replacement. Vehicles rated for over 6000 lb. GVW didn't need them, as the emissions regulations were less strict. Therefore, many buyers equipped their pickups, vans, Blazers, and Suburbans with heavier-duty suspensions that brought them up past 6000-lb. GVW.

Fleetside pickup and Blazer models featured a new quick-release tailgate that enabled the gate to be quickly and easily removed and re-installed. This feature was especially beneficial to owners who carried slide-in camper bodies on their pickups..

Aside from some horsepower shuffling due to ever-tightening emissions regulations, most Chevy trucks carried over with few changes for **1976.** Some of the changes included a newly optional automatic transmission for the little LUV pickup, stacked rectangular headlights for uplevel models of the El Camino (lower models kept round headlights), and a new "Vantastic" trim package for the Chevy Van. More significant was a new upper body structure on the Blazer SUV. Instead of the totally removable top, Blazers got a solid cab over the front seats—sort of a regular-cab pickup roof without a back window or rear panel. Behind that was either a fixed or removable "cap." Newly available on many models was a smaller V-8 of 305 cubic inches. Dropped from the lineup was the little Vega Express Panel.

Yet another year of minimal changes marked the **1977**

Chevrolet trucks, and apparently, they didn't need any more than that; calendar-year sales topped a million units for the second year in a row.

There were, however, some notable "firsts." The LUV line added a chassis-cab intended as a platform for a motorhome body, though it also hosted flat-bed and stake-bed bodies. One-ton pickups finally got optional 4WD (it had been available only in ½- and ¾-ton versions), and Blazers offered a soft-top option for the rear part of the body that could also be capped with a hard top.

Light-duty truck sales were at an all-time high as trucks accounted for one out of every three new vehicles sold by Chevrolet dealers. The greatest increase came from the personal-use market, with Blazer sales running about 33 percent ahead of their 1976 figure. One theory is that shoppers wanting something different used to buy sporty performance cars. But by the mid-'70s, "performance" was merely painted on, so they began gravitating toward trucks.

The Isuzu-built LUV truck got a facelift for **1978** that replaced its dual rectangular headlights with single round headlights flanking a restyled grille. A redesigned instrument panel was also new.

More extensive changes marked the El Camino for 1978. It was resized and restyled along with Chevrolet's entire midsize car line, which switched its name from "Chevelle" to "Malibu." The El Camino ended up nearly a foot shorter than before on a one-inch-longer wheelbase that now stretched to 117.1 inches. It retained the "flying buttress" roofline, but added small rear quarter windows. Front ends went to single square headlights flanking an upright, rectangular grille, and

the taillights were rectangular slots in the bumper, but the overall look was easily recognizable as an El Camino. The base engine was now a 200-cubic-inch V-6 producing 95 horsepower. Optional were a 105-hp 231-cid V-6, a 145-hp 305-cid V-8, and a 165-hp 350 V-8.

Chevy Vans got a revised grille and headlight treatment, but the conventional pickups—along with the Blazer and Suburban—returned virtually unchanged. However, newly optional on C10 ½-ton pickups was Chevrolet's first diesel engine, a normally aspirated (no turbocharger) 350-cubic-inch V-8 putting out 120 hp. The diesel was expected to increase overall fuel economy by 20 to 25 percent and was significantly more frugal when idling, both of which made it particularly well suited for fleet use.

Conventional pickups, Blazers, and Suburbans got a freshened front end for **1979,** but other models returned virtually unchanged in appearance. However, a small 267-cid V-8 was added as an option for the El Camino, and the LUV truck was newly available in a 4WD version.

Over the course of the decade, trucks of virtually every flavor—conventional and compact pickups, vans, and sport-utility vehicles—saw a significant rise in popularity, as they seemingly replaced stylish or performance-oriented cars as the "cool" vehicle to have. Toward the end of the '70s, in fact, Stepide pickups were increasingly chosen over the more practical Fleetside versions, a sop to the former's perceived "macho" look.

As it turned out, this trend toward trucks wasn't just a flash in the pan; it would continue to the end of the century, and well into the next.

1

3

4

2

5

1-2. A slightly revised grille texture with 12 sets of horizontal ribs was one of the subtle changes to the 1970 Chevrolet light-duty trucks. Top-of-the-line trim level was the CST/10 (CST stood for Custom Sport Truck, 10 for the ½-ton series). The upper belt molding seen on this example was optional, but all CST/10s got a wide lower-body molding and tailgate appliqué with wood-grain trim. **3-4.** An answer to the Jeep CJ and Ford Bronco, the Chevy Blazer arrived for 1969 with four-wheel drive only. It continued for 1970 with few changes, plus a new two-wheel-drive version. A bolt-on removable fiberglass top with integral locking liftgate allowed the Blazer to become a "roadster pickup" or, with the optional rear bench seat, an open-air fun machine with seating for five. **5.** Like their Fleetside siblings, Stepside pickups came with either 6½-foot (shown here) or 8-foot beds. A basic two-wheel-drive Stepside like this one started at $2520; the 8-foot bed version started at $40 more.

1

2

3

4

5

6

1. In the original sales brochure, Chevy said there was nothing like an El Camino. Period. It was true that El Camino had few peers. For 1970, the car-based pickup was redesigned up front to closely mimic its Chevelle parent. The SS 396 option added a "big block" V-8 engine, special hood, and sport wheels. **2.** A revised instrument panel was also new. **3.** A '70 El Camino SS 396 could be fitted with Strato-bucket seats, floor console, and a special instrument package with round gauges. **4.** Chevy's Conventional Series 40, 50, and 60 models came in a variety of single- and tandem-axle configurations, including this C/40 stake-bed. Tilt-cab models (background) came in Series 50 and 60. Their cabs pivoted forward 55 degrees to allow easy engine access. **5.** Chevy's heavy-duty tandem diesel models boasted up to 50,000 pounds Gross Vehicle Weight, and up to 76,800 pounds Gross Combined Weight. **6.** The short conventional-cab tractor's relatively compact wheelbase made it easier to maneuver in tight loading spaces.

Chevy goes heavy! New Titan 90.

Anybody could have added a new truck to their '70 lineup. Leave it to Chevrolet to add a truck and a half

New Titan 90.

Never before has a Chevy tilt been so long on muscle.

So right for turnpike stretches.

With any one of 9 diesels available to put under the driver when he's at the wheel. Or one of the biggest sleeping compartments on the road to put under him when he's not.

Conventionals. Vans. Recreational vehicles. Whatever you're thinking, your Chevrolet dealer's got it.

And it's a Mover.

Chevy goes lively! New '70 pickup.

The first thing a Chevy pickup has to move is you. And we never forget it.

It shows in the way our '70s look.

In their coil spring smoothness.

Car-like option lists.

Power choices.

And all the different ways they come: Fleetside, Stepside and camper-designed Longhorn (the second car that doubles as a second home).

Chevy goes anywhere! New

Call it Chevrolet's convertible-stat wagon-car-truck if you've got the tim call it Blazer for short.

Order it with removable hardtop.

wheel drive for telling trails to get los

Putting you first, keeps us first. CHEVR

On the move:
New Chevrolet Movers for '70.

1

2

3

1. An ad showcases the large and "small" of the 1970 "Chevy Movers" truck lineup. The heavy-duty Titan 90 tilt-cab semi truck was the new king of the hill. **2.** The 1971 El Camino looked plenty sporty in SS trim. This year's facelift included dual "Power Beam" headlights instead of 1970's quad units. El Camino SSs shared powertrains with their Chevelle siblings: a 350 V-8 with 245 or 270 horsepower or a 454 with 365 or 425 hp. Base package prices were also the same as for the cars at $357 and $385, respectively. **3.** Chevy's van was redesigned for 1971. The Chevy Van was available with a 110- or 125-inch wheelbase in ½-ton G-10, ¾-ton G-20, or one-ton G-30 models. Basic cargo vans and windowed passenger versions were available, each with a choice of inline six or V-8 engines. Standard passenger vans were dubbed Sportvan, and better-equipped versions wore Beauville badges. A 1972 Chevy Van is shown.

1

2

3

4

130 CLASSIC CHEVROLET TRUCKS

5

6

7

1-4. For 1972, ½-ton pickups were little changed and carried over the eggcrate grille that debuted for 1971. **5.** The Titan 90 remained Chevy's top-dog truck. Its base price could run up to $34,545 and its Gross Vehicle Weight ratings topped out at a whopping 50,500 pounds. **6.** Chevy entered the sub-compact game in 1971 with the Vega. It came in three body styles, including a slick little "Kammback" wagon that was also offered with blanked-out rear quarter windows as the Vega Panel Express. The 1972 model shown here started at $2152, but only 4114 were sold. **7.** Like its pickup counterpart, the Blazer sport-utility vehicle returned for 1972 with few changes.

1. Chevy redesigned its light-duty truck line for 1973 with more sculpted lines. The Blazer sport-utility was basically a short-chassis pickup. The optional "Sports Cap" roof was removable. **2.** The new Fleetside pickup was well-suited to hauling a camper. **3.** All the new light-duty trucks shared interior styling. A Blazer with the Cheyenne option is shown. **4.** Starting with the redesign, the big Suburban had two doors on each side. **5-6.** The El Camino was also restyled for '73.

1

2

1. Chevy's line of full-size trucks saw only minor changes in the mid-Seventies. The 1975 light-duties had new grilles, but otherwise looked little different. 2-3. Also virtually unchanged, the 1975 LUV was ready for work or play. Luxury Mikado trim dressed up the interior with touches like deluxe fabric, carpeting, deluxe dome lamps with door-operated switches, and nameplates. 4-5. Blazer looked little different for 1976, but there was actually a significant change. The front section of the cab now had a standard steel half top with a built-in roll bar. As a result, only the rear section of the roof that covered the rear seating or cargo bay was a removable fiberglass piece. 6. Blazer's available Cheyenne interior added leather-grained vinyl or custom cloth upholstery on the bucket seats. The package also included a console between the front seats, gauge-type instrumentation with simulated woodgrain trim, additional insulation, and color-keyed carpeting.

3

4

5

6

El Caminos were carried over with little change for 1977; this car-pickup's basic design dated back to 1973. The stacked quad headlights and vertical grille bars on this example identify it as an uplevel Classic model. Lesser versions had single round headlights and a rectangular grille pattern. El Camino Classics started at $4403 and weighed in at 3763 pounds. A 145-hp two-barrel 305 was the base V-8; a 170-hp four-barrel 350 was a $210 option. Eye-catching two-tone paint and sporty rally wheels were also optional.

1

2

1. Chevy pickups continued virtually unchanged for 1978. Shown is a C10 ½-ton in Scottsdale trim. With a base 305-cid V-8, C10 prices started at $4418 for a shortbed, or $4493 with long bed. Both were available with a Stepside cargo box at no extra cost.
2. The '78 Chevy Van (top right) received a handsome facelift that included a new grille and rectangular headlights. Vans were available in ½-ton G10 or ¾-ton G20 (shown) versions.
3. Chevy's trusty medium-duty trucks soldiered into 1978 with few changes. C65 models came standard with a 366-hp V-8. A conventional alligator-type hood or this tilt nose were available. 4. New for '78 was the Bruin line of big trucks (left), which had a contemporary styled fiberglass tilt hood and offered Detroit Diesel or Cummins diesel engines. Meanwhile, the 70-Series tractors (right) made do with the old styling.

3

4

1

2

3

4

6

5

1-3. The redesigned 1978 El Camino was once again based on Chevy's intermediate car line, so it carried the styling of the new, downsized Malibu. Engine choices ranged from a 3.3-liter V-6 to the 350-cid V-8. Shown here is the uplevel Conquista trim. A Super Sport version continued to be offered. Starting prices ranged from $3807 for a base V-6 model to $5022 for a V-8 SS. El Camino's similarity with Malibu also carried over to the interior. Chevy said the new intermediate design provided greater room and comfort despite smaller exterior dimensions. **4.** The LUV pickup soldiered into 1979 virtually unchanged. **5.** Also returning with few changes was the Beauville passenger van. **6.** Pickups now shared their grille with Blazers and Suburbans. **7.** Chevrolet's light-duty trucks, including the Blazer (shown) sport-utility vehicle, were still popular in 1979 and received only minor changes, including a slightly revised hood and grille along with a catalytic convertor to meet emissions requirements.

7

CHAPTER 7
1980-1989

A second oil crisis in 1979 drove up the price of gas and drove down the sales of larger vehicles, Chevrolet trucks among them. During 1980, total Chevy truck production dropped below one million units for the first time since 1976.

For better or worse, Chevrolet hadn't invested much in changes to its **1980** truck line. Conventional pickups, Blazers, Suburbans, and Chevy Vans all got revised grilles and rectangular headlights to replace round ones, but otherwise looked little different. However, engine choices were shuffled, lock-up torque converters were introduced, and radial tires and front air dams were fitted to some models, all in the interest of boosting fuel economy.

At the low end of Chevy's truck lineup, the little Isuzu-sourced LUV compact pickup and car-based El Camino pickup carried on virtually unchanged. At the opposite end, the big over-the-road Series 90 tractor only carried on a short way; it was discontinued at midyear.

The Isuzu-built LUV compact pickup was redesigned for **1981,** with smoothed-out front sheetmetal, rectangular headlights, a larger cab with 2½ inches more legroom, and a restyled interior, all on a two-inch-longer wheelbase. The powerplant of choice, however, remained the 111-cid four cylinder used since 1972.

El Caminos got a slightly revised grille treatment, but the biggest news was under the hood. All available engines were fitted with GM's Computer Command Control (CCC) carburetion, which helped them meet ever-tightening emissions requirements.

Front-end treatments were again revised for the full-size trucks (conventional pickups, Blazers, Suburbans) and the Chevy Van, which got stacked, dual rectangular headlights in place of the former single rectangular lights. Grilles also got a bolder texture.

With the big Series 90 tractor gone, Chevrolet put more emphasis on its medium-duty line. Since urban delivery trucks were leaning more and more toward diesel power, Chevrolet responded by offering a choice of three rugged mid-range diesel engines: Detroit Diesel's Fuel Pincher 8.2-liter naturally aspirated V-8, Caterpillar's 10.4-liter naturally

aspirated model 3208, and Cummins' 9.1-liter turbocharged model VT-225.

The big news for **1982** was the introduction of the American-built S-10 compact pickup. It was a bit larger than the Japanese-built LUV pickup and came with bigger engines; standard was an 82-hp 119-cid four, while a 110-hp 173-cid V-6 was optional. The LUV, meanwhile, remained in the lineup, adding a 58-hp 136-cid diesel to the existing 80-hp 111-cid four-cylinder gas engine. Also still offered was the car-based El Camino, which got little besides a revised grille flanked by dual rectangular headlights that replaced single square lights.

Full-size trucks, including the Blazer and Suburban, showed few changes for 1982—unless you ordered the optional diesel engine. In that case, what you got was GM's new 130-hp 6.2-liter (379 cubic inch) V-8 oil burner that replaced the former 125-hp 350-cid unit. The diesel was not offered in the unchanged Chevy Van—at least, not yet.

Diesel engines continued to gain favor in full-size trucks, so for **1983,** Chevrolet offered its 6.2-liter in Chevy Vans for the first time. This made them the only vans available with diesel power. Joining the diesel was a new four-speed automatic transmission, which was also new for the little-changed full-size pickups, Blazers, and Suburbans. The "old" 5.7-liter V-8 diesel was newly available in the El Camino, which was otherwise a virtual rerun.

But the biggest news for 1983 occurred in the S-10 line

introduced for 1982. At first offered only as a regular-cab 2WD pickup, the S-10 "expanded" to include an extended-cab version, along with adding an available 7.4-foot "long box" and optional 4WD. Another addition was the S-10 Blazer, a two-door sport-utility wagon that mimicked its pickup counterpart forward of the center roof pillar. Added to the S-10 engine roster was a 62-hp 136-cid four-cylinder diesel. With the S-10 now covering such a broad spectrum, the Isuzu-built LUV truck was relegated to history.

Few changes marked the **1984** lineup of Chevy trucks, as most models simply got revised trim and the usual altered color assortment. The El Camino carried on despite the fact that the car on which it was based—the Malibu—had been discontinued.

Chevrolet added the rear-wheel-drive Astro minivan to its lineup for **1985,** and also introduced electronic fuel injection and a couple of new engines.

The Astro was aimed at the phenomenally success-ful minivans introduced by Chrysler Corporation for 1984. Compared with the Dodge Caravan and Plymouth Voyager, Astro was somewhat larger—though not as large as a full-size van—was built on a traditional frame, had rear-wheel drive rather than front-wheel drive, and offered a V-6 engine rather than just a four cylinder. Initial engine choices were both new to the line. The smaller one was the "Iron Duke," a 2.5-liter four with single-point electronic fuel injection. This system was called Throttle Body Injection, or TBI. Also avail-

able was a 4.3-liter V-6 with four-barrel carburetor. The new 2.5 was offered in the S-10 line, and a 4.3 became the stan-dard engine for the El Camino and Chevy Van.

Full-size conventional trucks, including the Blazer and Suburban, came with a 305-cid V-8 as standard equipment; some models previously offered the now-defunct 250-cid six as the base engine. Otherwise, aside from some minor trim variations, all the full-size trucks carried into 1985 with few changes.

For **1986,** a TBI (fuel injected) version of the 4.3-liter V-6 called the Vortec was newly standard on full-size pickups and newly optional in the Astro. A similar TBI system was added to the 2.8-liter V-6 that was optional on the S-10 pick-up and Blazer. Those models also get a revised instrument panel and available Insta-Trac 4WD, which allowed shifting from 2WD to 4WD without having to come to a stop.

There were no changes of note to the full-size Blazer or Suburban, but the Chevy Van got optional 60/40 split swing-out side doors, and the El Camino got a revised instrument panel.

During the 1986 model year, nearly 600,000 car owners switched to trucks in order to meet particular passenger, cargo, and trailering needs. Interestingly, trucks also were becoming second and third family vehicles. A study by the University of Michigan's Survey Research Center found that while only 11 percent of main family vehicles were trucks, the second and third or fourth family vehicle was a truck in

40 percent of households surveyed.

Meanwhile, industry research showed that nearly 67 percent of consumers surveyed bought light trucks primarily for personal use, indicating their direct connection to what social commentators called "lifestyle choices."

The biggest news for **1987** was that electronic fuel injection—in the form of GM's Throttle Body Injection (TBI)—was made standard on all gasoline engines; previously, all the V-8s were carbureted. Otherwise, the full-size Blazer, Suburban, conventional pickups, and Chevy Van were virtual carry-overs.

The S-10 pickups and Blazer SUV—the latter being the most popular vehicle of its type in the country—gained a serpentine accessory belt for both the base 2.5-liter four-cylinder engine and the optional 2.8-liter V-6. Dropped from the engine roster was the never-popular four-cylinder diesel. Otherwise, there were few other changes. Ditto the Astro minivan. Also little-changed was the El Camino, which was in its last full model year; a few were built in early 1988 before this interesting and attractive car-based pickup was relegated to history.

1988 was a very big year for Chevrolet trucks. The headline news was that the pickups saw their first redesign in 15 years. Body sides were now smooth with a slight convex curve and subtle wheelwell flares. Two distinct front-end treatments were used. Upper-line models had side-by-side (rather than stacked) dual rectangular headlights that sat above equal-sized turn-signal lamps, somewhat retaining the look of the previous model but in a lower, more streamlined form. Base and mid-range models used single square headlights underlined by smaller turn-signal lamps, and typically had a painted rather than chrome front bumper.

Regular-cab wheelbases remained the same, but newly added was an extended cab that could seat up to six passengers with a rear bench seat that could be either fixed or folding. Extended cabs did not have separate rear doors—yet. Overall lengths were longer than before as cabs gained some front legroom, and also offered increased shoulder room inside despite being 3½-inches narrower outside. Instrument panels were also redesigned, with squared-off shapes and high-set audio and climate controls. A heavy-duty, four-door, six-passenger, long-bed Crew cab was still sold, but it continued in the old body style, essentially a carry-over 1987 model.

Both 6½-foot and eight-foot beds were again offered on the new trucks. The short bed came in straight-sided Fleetside form and also as the new Sportside. The latter was similar to a traditional Stepside bed except that the flared fenders were molded smoothly into the sides of the bed rather than being separate fenders that were tacked on. The Sportside bed was available only on regular-cab pickups, and unlike the Fleetside, wasn't offered in an eight-foot length.

Rear-wheel-drive models were again denoted with a "C"

prefix and came in ½- (1500), ¾- (2500), and one-ton (3500) versions. Four-wheel-drive models were identified similarly, but with a "K" prefix. They came with GM's Insta-Trac 4WD system that was not for use on dry pavement but could be switched in and out of 4WD "on the fly."

Powertrain choices didn't change much as all engines had gone to fuel injection the year before. The base 4.3-liter V-6 produced 160 hp; other choices included a 175-hp 5.0-liter V-8, 210-hp 5.7-liter V-8, 230-hp 7.4-liter V-8, and 143-hp 6.2-liter diesel V-8. Depending on the engine chosen, buyers could get a four- or five-speed manual transmission or a three- or four-speed automatic. Rear antilock brakes were standard.

Although the full-size Blazer and Suburban had traditionally been based on the full-size pickups, both these SUVs returned in their previous form. They lacked the pickups' rear antilock brakes and came standard with the 5.7-liter V-8. Both also offered the 6.2-liter diesel V-8, but only the Suburban could be ordered with the big 7.4-liter V-8—and then only in the ¾-ton (2500) version. Suburbans still offered a choice of side-by-side cargo doors or a tailgate arrangement; Blazers came only with the tailgate.

In the compact S-10 line, not much had changed when the 1988 models arrived, but at midyear, GM's 4.3-liter Vortec V-6 was added as an option. The existing 2.5-liter four and 2.8-liter V-6 carried on, giving buyers a wide range of engine choices.

The El Camino car-based pickup was dropped after a brief run of 1988 models, never (so far) to return. The Astro minivan and full-size Chevy Van carried on as virtual reruns.

After a rousing 1988, Chevrolet closed out the decade with a **1989** truck line that saw few changes. The full-size Blazer and Suburban SUVs continued with their "old" truck styling, still not adopting the bodywork of the redesigned full-size pickups. However, grilles and headlights were altered to mimic the look of the top-line pickups, with the same side-by-side dual rectangular headlights over "mirror image" turn-signal lamps.

S-10 pickups and Blazers added standard rear antilock brakes, as did the Astro minivan and full-size Chevy Van. Otherwise, those models carried on virtually unchanged.

One other event of 1989 deserves mention. Although they didn't carry the Chevrolet nameplate—yet—Chevrolet dealers began selling vehicles built by Isuzu, Suzuki, and a joint venture with Toyota under the Geo badge this year. One of these models was the little Suzuki-built Tracker SUV, a four-seat two-door in either hardtop wagon or convertible form with a 1.6-liter four-cylinder engine.

Bolstered by the success of its redesigned full-size pickups, Chevrolet closed out the 1980s with a fine product line that would get nothing but better in the Nineties.

1

2

5

3

4

6

1-2. As the 1980s dawned, Chevy's mainstay light-duty truck line saw few changes. This Blazer and Suburban display the main visual update: rectangular headlamps. Blazers remained exclusively a 4-wheel-drive offering, but the Suburban was offered in both rear-wheel- and 4-wheel-drive versions. **3.** Chevy's biggest rig, the Bison conventional, made its last appearance for 1980. The heavy-duty Chevrolet Titan cab-over was also discontinued. **4.** A Chevy truck staple since 1972, the compact LUV (Light Utility Vehicle) pickup, built by Izusu in Japan, was redesigned for 1981. **5-6.** The car-based El Camino continued to be a stylish alternative to the full-size pickup truck. For 1981, the grille carried horizontal rather than vertical bars, but otherwise there was little new.

1

2

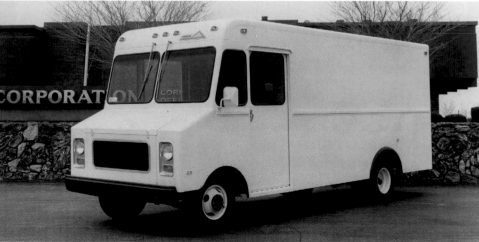

3

4

5

1-2. With Chevy out of the heavy-duty truck business, the medium-duties were the company's brawniest offerings. These trucks came in three conventional single-axle series—50, 60, and 70—as well as a tandem rear-axle Series 70. The Kodiak cab was optional on the mediums; it sat about seven inches higher than the standard cab and came with a fiberglass tilt hood. **3.** Chevy's 1982 Step Vans offered diesel power for the first time. Inline six-cylinder and V-8 gas engines were also available. **4.** This 1982 50 Series medium-duty truck wears the standard cab. With this cab style, an alligator-style hood was standard, but the truck shown here is equipped with the optional fiberglass tilt hood. **5.** Chevy's regular light-duty pickup line for 1982 wore the front-end styling introduced the previous year, but under the hood there was a newly optional 6.2-liter diesel engine. Here it is joined on the track by its new made-in-America little brother, the 1982 S-10. The S-10 was larger than the LUV and came in 108- and 118-inch-wheelbase versions. Four-cylinder power was standard, but a V-6 was offered at extra cost.

1983
CHEVY
MEDIUMS

HEAVY-DUTY
PAYLOADS WITHOUT
HEAVY-DUTY PRICES

TOUGH CHEVY TRUCKS ARE TAKING CHARGE

CHEVY TRUCKS

1

2

3

148 CLASSIC CHEVROLET TRUCKS

4

5

1-3. Chevy's medium-duty line boasted more optional CAT 3208 diesel engines for 1983, along with a new Spicer five-speed manual transmission for C70 conventionals. Standard and Kodiak cabs remained available. **4-6.** For 1983, the El Camino carried on with the four-headlamp appearance that was new the previous year. By this time, it (along with its GMC Caballero twin) was America's only car-based pickup. Prices started at $8191. **7-8.** Chevy's light-duty trucks had a new grille for 1983, but little else changed. **9.** Perhaps the biggest news for 1983 was the new S-10 Blazer. A logical spinoff of the S-10 pickup, the new sport-utility vehicle used the same powertrains, chassis, front sheetmetal, and dashboard, but substituted an enclosed cargo area behind the doors. Sales were strong, as buyers appreciated the "baby Blazer's" superior mileage and handling versus the full-size Blazer.

6

7

8

9

1

2

3

1. For 1984, Chevy added the medium-duty Tiltmaster. This low-cab-forward tilt-cab line was built by Isuzu Motors Ltd. of Japan. **2.** Chevy responded to Chrysler Corporation's 1984 front-drive minivan with the rear-drive Astro for 1985. Somewhat larger and heavier than the Chrysler minis, the Astro was available with a 2.5-liter four-cylinder or a 4.3-liter V-6. **3.** Chevy pickups, like this 1986 model, remained strong sellers despite only minor year-to-year changes. **4.** Beauville remained Chevy's top-line full-size van for '86. **5.** Also in 1986, Chevy dealers sold an El Camino SS fitted with a "droop snoot" that mimicked the nose on the company's popular Monte Carlo SS. **6.** Ritzy Silverado trim dresses up this 1987 K-10 Stepside 4×4. **7.** For 1987, Chevy still offered a complete line of medium duties.

4

6

5

7

1

3

2

1. Chevy finally refreshed the full-size pickup line for 1988. This grille and headlamp treatment was exclusive to the top-line Silverado trim. **2.** Buyers were demanding more interior room and storage, and Chevy obliged for '88 with two-door extended cabs in most configurations. **3.** Sportside was the new name for flared-fender full-sized Chevy pickups. Base Cheyennes and mid-level Scottsdales used one headlamp per side. **4.** Bigger-than-life bodyside 4×4 graphics were available on the 1989 K-series full-size pickups. **5.** The big Blazer (shown) and Suburban carried on with the circa-1973 design, but a new grille introduced for 1989 made them look more like the new pickups. **6.** Also still using the old design were the heavy-duty pickups like this 1989 Crew Cab with dual rear wheels. **7.** The S10 Cameo was a dealer-installed appearance package.

4

6

5

7

CHAPTER 8

1990-1999

Chevrolet entered the 1990s the number-two light-truck maker behind Ford, but that just seemed to make the bowtie team try harder. New models were added and existing lines expanded in Chevy's quest for number one.

Although Chevrolet already had the rear-drive Astro minivan, the company added the front-drive Lumina APV to its lineup for **1990.** Based on the automotive platform of the Lumina sedan and coupe, the APV (All Purpose Vehicle) had plastic-composite body panels and wore a sloping, pointed nose that earned it the "Dustbuster" nickname. The only powertrain offered was a 120-hp 3.1-liter V-6 and three-speed automatic. In back was a traditional liftgate cargo door. A similar minivan was sold by Pontiac as the Trans Sport and Oldsmobile as the Silhouette, but only the Lumina APV came in a cargo version.

Updating the Astro were standard four-wheel antilock brakes and a new all-wheel-drive option, the first of its kind in a minivan. At midyear came an extended version of the Astro, which had the same wheelbase but added 10 inches of length behind the rear wheels for increased cargo capacity.

Also adding a stretched version was the full-size Chevy Van. It rode a 146-inch wheelbase vs. 110- and 125-inch spans. Rear-wheel ABS was now standard.

In the S-10 line, Blazers now came standard with the 4.3-liter V-6 that could be newly mated to a five-speed manual transmission in addition to the existing four-speed automatic.

Filling out the full-size pickup line for 1990 were the high-performance, limited-edition 454 SS pickup and a WT (Work Truck) 1500, a stripped, regular-cab "workhorse." The 454 SS carried a 230-hp 7.4-liter (454-cid) V-8, three-speed automatic transmission, lower rear-axle ratio (it came only in 2-wheel drive), and a sport suspension with meaty tires.

Meanwhile, the full-size Blazer and Suburban got standard rear-wheel antilock brakes. They were both still based on the "old" (1973-1987) pickup design, having yet to follow the lead of the redesigned pickup that arrived for 1988.

After a rather busy 1990, Chevrolet's truck line generally saw few changes for **1991** aside from minor trim variations. There were some exceptions, however. The compact SUV segment was growing by leaps and bounds, and to counter a four-door Explorer due from Ford and an existing four-door Jeep Cherokee, the S-10 Blazer added a four-door version in the spring of 1990 as a 1991 model. It initially came only in 4-wheel-drive form, and like all S-10 Blazers, came standard with the 4.3-liter V6.

For **1992,** Chevrolet's bright spot in SUV sales was in full-size models; the Suburban and Blazer posted impressive increases over 1991. One reason was that both of these models finally adopted the styling of the contemporary pickups, which had been redesigned for 1988. In the process, Blazer gained five inches in wheelbase, four-wheel antilock brakes, and 1000 lb. in towing capacity, now 7000 lb. Blazer

came standard with 4WD. The Suburban also got four-wheel ABS and continued to offer both panel doors in the rear or a liftglass/tailgate arrangement. Half- and ¾-ton models continued in both two- and four-wheel-drive form, and passenger models could seat up to nine.

The one-ton four-door Crew Cab pickup also finally switched over to the new pickup styling, gaining four inches in wheelbase. Diesel engine choices expanded to include a new 190-hp 6.5-liter turbodiesel V-8, which joined the carry-over 130-hp 6.2-liter diesel V-8.

On Astro vans, four-wheel ABS was now standard on all but the cargo versions. Astros also got a midyear horsepower boost, going from 170 to 200, and were rated to tow up to 6000 lb. Another midyear change was an available "Dutch door" cargo-door setup, which had a one-piece liftglass on the top half and side-by-side doors on the lower half.

Lumina APVs gained four-wheel antilock brakes as standard equipment. Added as an option was a 165-hp 3.8-liter V-6 and four-speed automatic transmission, a combination that raised maximum towing capacity from 2000 lb. to 3000.

The G-Series full-size vans, the cargo version of which was formerly called "Chevy Van," got a revised grille.

There were no changes of note on the S-10 pickups, but the S-10 Blazer got four-wheel ABS and a revised 4WD system that allowed changing from 2WD to 4WD High or Low with the push of a button rather than the shifting of a lever.

One development that worked in favor of Chevrolet—and the Big Three in general—was the loss of market share by

Japanese light trucks over the previous six years. Japanese brands peaked in 1986 with 20.4 percent of the U.S. light-truck market. By 1992 that figure had dropped to 13.5 percent, the same share Japanese brands had in 1982.

GM's new 4L60-E electronically controlled four-speed automatic transmission was newly offered on most rear-wheel-drive trucks for **1993**. It allowed more precise shift control than the hydraulic transmission it replaced.

Most other changes to Chevrolet trucks for 1993 were relatively minor. However, the Lumina APV gained a power-sliding side door; the Astro got an optional driver-side air-bag midyear, and the cargo version got the four-wheel ABS already fitted to its passenger siblings; and availability of the 6.5-liter turbodiesel was expanded to include ¾-ton full-size pickups instead of just one-ton models. Also, this year proved to be the last for the G-Series-based Hi-Cube model that offered boxy 10- and 12-foot bodies, and also the big Step Van, which had been popular for urban deliveries.

The early 1990s was a good time to be in the truck business. Overall truck sales expanded from 33 percent of the U.S. market in 1989 to 39 percent in 1993, and continued to head upward.

Chevrolet introduced a redesigned S-10 pickup for **1994,** though its S-10 Blazer sibling carried on virtually unchanged. The pickup had fresh styling that featured a rounded front end, and came standard with a new 118-hp 2.2-liter four. Rear antilock brakes were standard, but four-wheel ABS came with the optional 4.3-liter V-6. Regular and extended cabs were offered; the former came with a 6.1- or 7.4-foot bed, the latter only with the shorter bed. Two special models

debuted: the SS, a 2WD with the 4.3 V-6 and sport suspension, and the ZR2 4WD with off-road styling.

Chevy's rear-drive Astro minivan got a standard driver-side airbag for 1994. So did the front-drive Lumina, which also got a new name—Lumina Minivan rather than Lumina APV—along with a restyled nose that was shorter and more blunt than before.

The full-size Blazer SUV added an optional 180-hp 6.5-liter turbodiesel V-8. So did the Suburban, though only on ¾-ton 2500 models. A non-turbo 6.5-liter diesel was newly available in the G-Series full-size van, which dropped its short-wheelbase version but added a standard driver-side airbag on light-duty models. Full-size pickups could now be ordered with either the turbo or non-turbo diesel engine.

The S-10 Blazer was redesigned for **1995** to match its pickup linemate, but wasn't called "S-10 Blazer" anymore; it was just "Blazer," as the full-size SUV that previously carried the name switched to "Tahoe." The new Blazer got a driver-side airbag in its redesigned interior.

By the same token, the S-10 pickup also dropped its "S-10" prefix, now taking the name "S-Series pickup." It also got a driver-side airbag for '95.

The Astro minivan lost its standard-length version but gained a facelift. The Lumina minivan carried on with few changes.

Among Chevy's full-size trucks, the pickups now came standard with four-wheel ABS and a driver-side air-bag. Suburbans also got the driver's airbag, along with a revamped dashboard. What had been the Blazer was renamed Tahoe, and it added a four-door version that slotted in size between the two-door model and the big Suburban, with which it shared the revised dash and driver-side airbag.

Virtually every truck in Chevrolet's lineup saw at least moderate revisions for **1996.** For the first time since 1971, the full-size van was completely redesigned. Passenger models were called "Express," cargo models simply "Van." As before, two sizes were offered, each gaining about 10 inches in wheelbase and 15 inches in overall length. Buyers had a choice of a sliding side door or 60/40 side-by-side doors. A revised interior featured dual airbags. The standard 4.3-liter V-6 returned, and the optional gas V-8s saw substantial power increases as they became part of Chevy's Vortec family of engines; the 5.0 was up 45 hp to 220, the 5.7 gained 50 hp to 250, the 7.4 put on 60 hp to 290. Also offered was a 190-hp 6.5-liter turbodiesel.

Full-size pickups got the same V-8 engine updates, and an available third door was added to the passenger side of the extended-cab short-bed version. It was hinged at the rear and didn't open independently; the front door had to be opened first.

The Suburban's standard 5.7-liter V-8 and optional (on 2500) 7.4-liter V-8 also got the Vortec treatment, and the available 4WD system gained push-button actuation. Tahoe's standard 5.7 V-8 did likewise, plus the line added a 2WD two-door model.

Among smaller offerings, the Astro got a revised dash with dual airbags, while the Lumina replaced its 3.1- and 3.8-liter V-6s with a lone 180-hp 3.4-liter V-6 in what was destined to be its final year in this form. The Blazer offered a permanently engaged all-wheel-drive system and its 4.3-liter V-6 got the Vortec treatment for '96, as did the V-6 in the S-Series pickups. The pickups also got an optional six-foot Sportside flare-fendered bed, while extended-cabs added an available third door on the driver's side.

With all that was new and improved, it's perhaps not surprising that Chevrolet had another record year of truck sales in 1996, as light-duty deliveries increased to 1,481,879 from 1,414,222 in 1995.

Chevy's redesigned front-drive minivan that appeared for **1997** also got a new name: Venture. Unlike the Lumina it replaced, the Venture had a conventional steel body rather than one of composite plastic. It came in two lengths; the shorter one was two inches longer in wheelbase but five inches shorter overall than the Lumina, while the extended version had an eight-inch-longer wheelbase and was 14 inches longer. Dual airbags were standard, as was a 180-hp 3.4-liter V-6. New options included a driver-side sliding side door and a power passenger-side sliding door.

Other models showed only minor changes. Light-duty versions of the full-size pickups, vans, Suburbans, and Tahoes all gained a standard passenger-side airbag, while the Astro got optional leather upholstery and the Blazer and S-Series pickup added an optional floor shifter for the automatic transmission.

Chevrolet absorbed the Geo lineup for **1998,** and that brought the Tracker compact SUV into the bowtie brigade. Tracker was built by Suzuki in Canada and offered in two-door convertible and four-door wagon form; the wagon was

11 inches longer in wheelbase and 15 inches longer overall than the tiny convertible. Dual front airbags were standard with ABS optional. The only engine was a 95-hp 1.6-liter four. It came standard with a five-speed manual transmission, while a three-speed automatic was optional on the convertible, a four-speed optional on the wagon.

The S-Series pickup reverted back to the S-10 name, and both it and the Blazer got a revised grille and headlights along with a passenger-side airbag. Blazer also got standard four-wheel ABS but lost its available "all surface" AWD system, leaving just conventional part-time 4WD that shouldn't be left engaged on dry pavement.

The Astro minivan got only minor revisions, but the Venture added standard front side airbags, an available driver-side sliding door for the short-wheelbase version (the long one already offered it), and optional OnStar assistance system. Among full-size models, the pickups returned virtually unchanged, as did the vans, but both the Suburban and Tahoe got available AutoTrac full-time 4WD and also offered OnStar.

A redesigned full-size pickup was the big news for **1999**. Newly named the Silverado, it came only in 1500 (½-ton) and 2500 (¾-ton) versions with a more rounded front end that carried much the same look as the older model. Wheelbases were up by about two inches, overall lengths by about nine inches. Regular and extended cabs were offered, the latter with a standard passenger-side third door. Beds choices included 6.5-foot Fleetside and Sportside (flare fendered) styles and an 8.1-foot Fleetside. Engine choices

started with the returning 4.3-liter V-6, but the V-8s were new, and included a 255-hp 4.8, a 270-hp 5.3, and a 300-hp 6.0. The last was offered only in the 2500 model, which could also be had with a 6.5-liter turbodiesel.

Oddly, select versions of the "old" pickup, also known as the C/K Series (C was for 2WD models, K for 4WD), continued to be sold alongside the Silverado. For '99, this was the only way to get a heavy-duty ¾-ton or one-ton pickup.

The smallest Chevy truck also made a big splash. Tracker switched its surname from Geo to Chevrolet in 1998, and both the two-door convertible and four-door wagon were redesigned for '99. Front ends were rounder and more "aero," and though wheelbases remained the same, overall length grew five inches on the convertible, one inch on the wagon. The latter got a larger 2.0-liter four-cylinder engine with 127 hp, which was optional on the convertible in place of a 97-hp 1.6.

AutoTrac AWD could be newly ordered on the Blazer, and the S-10 pickup replaced the SS model with an even more sporting Xtreme package that included ground-effect spoilers. The Venture minivan got an eight-passenger seating option, but other models, including the Astro and the full-size vans, Suburban, and Tahoe, returned virtually unchanged.

During the decade, Chevy trucks made huge strides in adopting safety features such as dual front airbags and ABS. They also added convenience features that made them ever more popular as a substitute for cars. Further advances in both areas would increase this popularity as the new millennium began.

1

2

3

4

5

6

7

1-5. For 1990, Chevrolet released this hot 454 SS version of its popular full-size pickup. Exclusively wearing Onyx Black paint, all 454 SS trucks were regular-cab, short-box Fleetsides with a big 230-horsepower 454-cubic-inch V-8 under the hood. **6.** Chevy added a second minivan for 1990, the front-wheel-drive Lumina APV. **7.** The new decade also introduced a fresh medium-duty offering, the Kodiak, in tractor and straight-truck versions. Kodiaks had a tilting fiberglass hood and could be fitted with gas or diesel engines. **8.** Chevy added an extended-length Astro van for 1990 (1991 model shown below). This model was 10 inches longer on an unchanged wheelbase.

8

1

2

3

4

5

6

1. A 1991 S-10 is shown equipped with the off-road-flavored Baja package. Note the (barely visible) bed-mounted spare tire. **2.** This was the last year the Suburban used the body introduced for 1973. **3-4.** Chevy's full-size pickups entered 1991 with few changes. **5.** In the spring of 1990, Chevy introduced a four-door S-10 Blazer as a 1991 model. **6.** The extended version of the 1992 Sportvan rode a 146-inch wheelbase. **7.** The full-size Blazer (shown) and Suburban were redesigned for 1992, finally adopting the styling the division's contemporary pickups had been using since 1988. Blazers sported standard four-wheel antilock brakes, 4-wheel drive, and a 7000-pound towing capacity. **8.** For 1992, the one-ton four-door Crew Cab pickup (K-3500 shown) finally switched to the new pickup styling.

7

8

1

1. Chevy's new Camaro Z28 served as the Official Pace Car of the 1993 Indianapolis 500. The company also supplied the Official Truck that wore the same paint scheme as the Camaro that paced the race. **2.** Chevy's popular full-size pickups looked largely the same for 1993, but there were some changes. The mid-level Scottsdale trim was discontinued, but most models were available with a newly optional four-speed overdrive automatic transmission. It featured electronic controls and a second-gear start feature for better take-offs on slippery surfaces. Also, a Sport Appearance Package (shown) was available exclusively for Sportside models. Alloy wheels and body-color grille and bumpers were included in the package.

2

1

2

3

1. This 1993 S-10 regular-cab long bed has the optional 4-wheel-drive system and Tahoe trim. The 4WD system was an on-demand, part-time system that Chevy called Insta-Trac. The S-10 saw few changes this year, but there was a new automatic transmission and a revised interior. **2.** For 1994, Chevy's front-drive minivan wore a restyled front end and a new name: Lumina Minivan. Other additions included an optional power opening and closing side door, extra-cost integral child seats, and a standard driver-side airbag. The base engine was a 120-horsepower 3.1-liter V-6, but a 170-horse 3.8-liter V-6 was also available. **3.** The big news for 1994 was a redesigned line of S-10 pickups. The ZR2 (shown) was a new off-road package that gave 4WD regular cab models a wider track, higher stance, and unique tires.

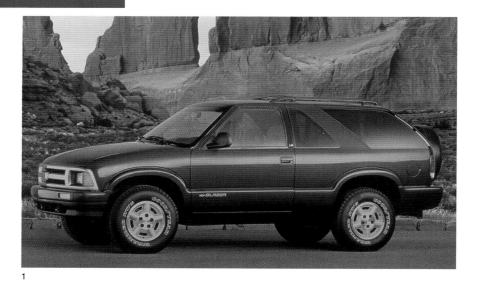

1

2

1-2. Chevy's compact SUV dropped its S-10 prefix to become simply the "Blazer" for 1995 and shared its basic design with the 1994 S-10 compact pickup. Both two- and four-door models were available. **3.** Detail changes were the only news for the '95 Suburban, still on a king-size 131.5-inch wheelbase. **4.** The big Chevy van, here a Sportvan Beauville, was little changed for 1995. This was the last year it used the basic design introduced for 1971. **5.** The Astro van received a facelift for 1995 and was now only available with the extended-length body. **6-7.** The full-size Blazer was renamed Tahoe for '95, and this new four-door version wore the same moniker. Riding a 117.5-inch wheelbase, the four-door Tahoe slotted between its two-door sibling and the Suburban in size.

3

4

5

6

7

1

2

3

5

1. A modified C-1500 served as the Official Pace Truck for the 1995 Brickyard 400 stock car race at the Indianapolis Motor Speedway. **2.** NASCAR added a series for race-modified pickups in 1995. Shown is a prototype of Chevy's entry. **3.** Chevy's big van was redesigned for 1996. Dubbed Express, the new line included a basic cargo van (white) and passenger models with long (red) or standard bodies. **4.** Big Chevy SUVs, like this Suburban LS, were little changed for 1997. **5.** Full-size extended-cab pickups added an optional third door for '96. **6.** Chevy's popular police car, the Caprice sedan, was discontinued after the 1996 model run, so Chevy showed this concept Tahoe Police Package in 1997 to float the idea of an SUV-based cruiser.

4

6

1

2

3

4

5

1. Chevy's front-drive Venture (center) replaced the Lumina Minivan for 1997.
2. If a 3500 Series truck wasn't tough enough, buyers could move up to an HD model, like this 1998 chassis-cab. 3. The S-10 pickup and related Blazer SUV (LT four-door shown) received a new face for '98. 4-5. Previously sold under the Geo brand, the compact Tracker two- and four-door SUVs wore the Chevy badge starting with the 1998 models. 6. For 1998, the increasingly popular Tahoe added Autotrac "full-time" 4-wheel drive that could be used on any surface. 7. Chevy produced a Police Package version of the rear-drive Tahoe, shown here as a 1998 model. In the end, the truck-based cruiser didn't prove to be as popular with law-enforcement agencies as the old Caprice sedan.

6

7

1

1. For 1999, Chevy's full-size pickup was redesigned for the first time in eleven years. At first, only 1500- and 2500-Series models were available. Extended-cab versions included a third door on the passenger side.
2. Silverado also offered a short Sportside bed. 3. A popular combination for heavy chores was a regular-cab Silverado 2500 4×4 with the long Fleetside bed. 4. The 1999 Tahoe (shown) and Suburban retained the previous design. 5. For 1999, 2WD S-10s were available with a sporty Xtreme package that included a "lowrider" suspension and lower-body skirts. 6-7. The Suzuki-built Tracker convertible and wagon were restyled for '99.

2

3

4

5

6

7

CHAPTER 9

2000-2009

Although Chevrolet and its GM parent entered the new millennium on a high note, both would face unprecedented challenges by the end of its first decade.

By this time, Chevy's light-duty truck lineup started with the adopted Tracker compact SUV formerly sold under the Geo nameplate and reached into one-ton pickups and vans—and beyond that with a range of medium-duty trucks. For the **2000** model year, the company offered a compact SUV, a midsize SUV, three large SUVs, a compact pickup, two styles of full-size pickups, a pair of minivans, and a full-size van. No other company had such a diverse light-duty lineup.

New for 2000 was a redesigned Tahoe and Suburban, Chevy's big SUVs. Tahoe abandoned its two-door version, the remaining four-door gaining an optional third-row seat for up to nine-passenger capacity to essentially become a 20-inch-shorter Suburban. However, the Suburban offered substantially more interior and cargo room and came in both ½- and ¾-ton versions, the latter offering an exclusive 300-hp 6.0-liter V-8. All the engines were new to these big people movers. Tahoe started with a 275-hp 4.8-liter V-8 and was available with a 285-hp 5.3, which was standard on Suburban. Dropped from the Suburban roster were the big 7.4-liter V-8 and the 6.5-liter turbodiesel. Rear-drive was standard, while 4-wheel-drive models used GM's Autotrac full-time system.

Chevy also carried over a couple of versions of the 1995-1999 Tahoe as 2000 models. The Z71 had off-road-oriented equipment with Autotrac 4WD, while the Limited was

a rear-wheel-drive model with Police Package equipment (heavy-duty suspension and brakes) and ground-effects spoilers. Both were four-door versions with a 255-hp 5.7-liter V-8.

Full-size ½-ton (1500) and light-duty ¾-ton (2500) pickups carried on after their 1999 redesign that brought fresh styling, new engines, and a fourth door for extended-cab models. Engine choices included a 200-hp 4.3-liter V-6 along with the same 4.8-, 5.3-, and 6.0-liter V-8s offered in Suburbans, the last in ¾-ton 2500 models only. Four-wheel-drive versions got GM's full-time Autotrac system. Buyers had a choice of 6.5- and eight-foot Fleetside beds or a 6.5-foot flare-fendered Sportside bed.

Also carried over for 2000 were the "old" heavy-duty pickups, the 2500 HD ¾-ton and 3500 one-ton, both based on the 1988-1998-style truck. They were offered in regular cab, extended cab (without rear doors), and four-door crew-cab form.

Rounding out Chevy's selection of full-size vehicles was the little-changed van. Passenger models could carry up to 15 people and were called the Express, cargo versions the Express Cargo Van. They were offered in ½-, ¾-, and one-ton versions in regular and extended length.

The Blazer continued as Chevy's midsize SUV in two- and four-door versions and with 2- or 4-wheel drive, the latter available with either part-time Insta-Trac or GM's full-time Autotrac system. The only engine was a 190-hp 4.3-liter V-6.

While the Blazer was offered in similar form as the GMC Jimmy and Oldsmobile Bravada, the little Tracker SUV

was a Chevy exclusive. For 2000, it carried over virtually unchanged after its 1999 redesign, and was still available in two-door convertible or four-door wagon form with 2- or 4-wheel drive and a choice of 1.6- and 2.0-liter four-cylinder engines.

Chevy continued to offer two distinct minivans for 2000. The first was the Astro, available with rear- or full-time 4WD. It now came standard with eight-passenger seating (seven with two center-row bucket seats) and carried over its 190-hp 4.3-liter V-6 and four-speed automatic transmission with Tow/Haul mode that helped it achieve a 5500-lb. towing capacity. Meanwhile, the front-drive Venture minivan continued with its 185-hp 3.4-liter V-6 and available 3500-lb. towing capacity. There were no more three-door Venture models for 2000; all came with dual sliding side doors. New was a Warner Bros. edition that included a rear-seat VCR entertainment system. Both the Astro and Venture were also offered in cargo versions.

Last but not least was the S-10 pickup, which carried over from 1999 virtually unchanged. Regular and extended cabs were offered, the latter with an optional third door on the driver's side. Six- and 7.3-foot Fleetside beds were available, along with a six-foot Sportside bed. Engine choices included a 120-hp 2.2-liter four and a 180-190-hp 4.3-liter V-6. Rear drive was standard, part-time 4WD optional. Returning were the Xtreme, a sporty, low-slung 2WD model, and the ZR2, a high-riding 4WD.

Chevy's biggest news for **2001**—quite literally—was a line of redesigned heavy-duty 2500 HD (¾-ton) and 3500 (one-ton) pickups that finally adopted the styling of the lighter-duty pickups introduced for 1999. Regular, extended, and crew-cab models returned; the extended now had dual rear-hinged back doors. Engine choices included a 325-hp 6.0-liter V-8, a 340-hp 8.1-liter V-8, and a new 300-hp 6.6-liter Duramax turbodiesel V-8. New for the 8.1 and 6.6 turbodiesel were a six-speed manual transmission and a five-speed Allison automatic. Four-wheel-drive models could get GM's Autotrac full-time system, and all 3500s came with dual rear wheels.

Half-ton Silverados added a crew-cab version called the 1500 HD (Heavy-Duty) with a standard 6.0-liter V-8; previously, the lightest crew cab offered was in the 2500 HD series. Newly optional on 2WD 1500s was traction control, a first for full-size pickups. Also new was a 6.5-foot composite Fleetside cargo bed that could be ordered on Z71 4WD extended cabs.

Also adding a crew-cab body style was the compact S-10 pickup; it came with a 4.6-foot bed. Dropped from the model offerings was the 4WD regular cab.

On the van front, Astros returned virtually unchanged, but the Venture got a stowable third-row seat. Late in the model year, Venture added a power-sliding driver-side door; a power-sliding passenger-side door was already offered. Full-size Express and Express Cargo Van returned with few changes, though an 8.1-liter V-8 was newly optional on one-ton versions to replace a 7.5-liter V-8.

Among Chevy's broad lineup of SUVs, the Tracker

dropped its 1.6-liter four and added a 155-hp 2.5-liter V-6 option to its wagon, the Blazer got a low-riding 2WD Xtreme model, and the Tahoe and Suburban gained GM's OnStar assistance system as an option. Not returning were the Z71 and Limited models of the 1995-99 design generation.

Two new model introductions marked Chevy's **2002** model year. First, a pickup version of the Suburban was launched as the Avalanche. In many ways, it was similar to a crew-cab pickup, but the bed was integral with the rest of the body, and between the two was a "midgate" that could be lowered and the rear glass removed to effectively expand the 5.3-foot bed to 8.1 feet. The innovative design also included storage compartments in the bed. Two- and four-wheel-drive versions were offered in ½- and ¾-ton models, the latter with an 8.1-liter V-8.

The second addition was the TrailBlazer, a bigger mid-size SUV. It originally came only in five-passenger form, but an extended version on a 16-inch-longer wheelbase arrived soon after that could seat up to seven. A new 270-hp 4.2-liter inline six was the only engine, but customers had a choice of 2WD or GM's full-time Autotrac 4WD.

Remaining in the line was an unchanged Blazer, now billed as a less-expensive midsize SUV option. Below that was the compact Tracker, also unchanged for 2002. At the top end were the Tahoe and Suburban, both being changed only in that many optional features were made standard, greatly increasing base prices.

An interesting new option was added for 1500 and 2500

Silverados at midyear. Called Quadrasteer, it turned the rear wheels counter to the fronts at low speeds to tighten the turning radius, and in the same direction as the fronts at higher speeds to increase stability. It came with a special flare-fendered cargo bed but also a steep $4500 price tag. As such, it didn't garner many orders, despite the fact it worked very well. Heavy-duty 2500 HD and 3500 pickups were little changed.

In other pickup news, the S-10 lost its long 7.3-foot bed, leaving regular and extended cabs with a six-foot bed in either Fleetside or Sportside form. Also offered was the four-door crew cab with a 4.6-foot bed introduced for 2001.

An all-wheel-drive system called Versatrak was added as an option to the Venture minivan for 2002, and the Warner Bros. edition swapped its VCR player for a DVD unit. There were only detail changes to Chevy's other vans, the Astro and Express.

It arrived late to the **2003** model-year party, but the new SSR instantly made big news. Based on the chassis and running gear of a 2WD TrailBlazer SUV, the SSR combined retro styling (mimicking Chevy's 1948-53 pickups) with a fascinating Rube Goldberg folding hardtop and five-foot cargo bed with rigid tonneau cover to create a unique, two-seat, hardtop-convertible pickup. Only one powertrain was offered: a 300-hp 5.3-liter V-8 and four-speed automatic transmission. At $41,370 it wasn't cheap, but it was surprisingly practical, and there was nothing else like it on the road.

It was otherwise a year of mostly carryover models,

though there were some notable exceptions. Silverado pickups—both light- and heavy-duty versions—got a revised grille and added a DVD entertainment option. New in the 1500 series was the SS, an AWD extended-cab short bed with a potent 345-hp 6.0-liter V-8 plus sport suspension and 20-inch wheels. Meanwhile, the smaller S-10 added an optional power sunroof for regular and extended cabs.

Also getting significant changes was the full-size Express van. All-wheel drive was a new option, as were left-side swing-out cargo doors, while a five-inch-longer nose gave it a fresh look. Astro and Venture minivans were virtual carryovers, though the formerly standard ABS was made optional on both, and front side airbags went from standard to optional on the Venture.

Chevy's big SUVs, the Tahoe and Suburban, gained optional adjustable pedals, DVD entertainment, and GM's Stabilitrak antiskid system. Both also moved front side airbags from standard to optional. Added for Suburban 2500s was the same Quadrasteer four-wheel steering system offered on Silverados.

Among the smaller SUVs, Tracker and Blazer saw only minor changes, while the TrailBlazer got optional DVD entertainment and added an available 290-hp 5.3-liter V-8. As was the case with its bigger brothers, TrailBlazer's front side airbags went from standard to optional.

Headlining news for **2004** was a new compact pickup. Called the Colorado, it was slightly larger than the S-10 and offered two new engines. Replacing a 120-hp 2.2-liter four as standard was a 175-hp 2.8-liter four. Available in place of the 190-hp 4.3-liter V-6 was a 220-hp 3.5-liter inline five-cylinder engine; both of the new engines were of double-overhead-cam design and based on the 4.2-liter inline six used in the TrailBlazer SUV. Cab choices included regular, extended with dual rear-hinged back doors, and four-door crew cab. As before, 2WD was standard, a part-time 4WD system optional. The crew cab had a five-foot bed, the others a six-foot bed. ABS was standard and curtain side airbags for all seating rows were optional. Also optional were traction control for 2WD models and GM's OnStar assistance system. Although Colorado effectively replaced the S-10, the latter was still offered in a lone 4WD crew-cab version as a less-expensive alternative to its Colorado counterpart.

Other changes for 2004 were less dramatic. The Avalanche added available Stabilitrak antiskid system for 2WD models, and the Silverado got a 1500 Crew cab with a 5.8-foot bed and 5.3-liter V-8; the former 1500 HD crew cab, which had a 6.5-foot bed and a 6.0-liter V-8, was moved up into the 2500 series. Also, the TrailBlazer got optional adjustable pedals and navigation system, the Tahoe and Suburban added a tire-pressure monitor, and the Tracker forfeited its two-door convertible and four-cylinder engine leaving only a V-6 wagon with 2- or 4-wheel drive. Express 3500 15-passenger vans got standard Stabilitrak antiskid system while cargo versions offered new pop-up access panels where the side windows would normally be. Astro, Blazer, SSR, Silverado HD, and Venture returned virtually unchanged.

A new vehicle was added for **2005** to strengthen Chevy's presence in the popular midsize SUV category. Called the Equinox, it was based on a front-drive automotive platform but also available in an all-wheel-drive version. It offered seating for five, with second-row seats that could move fore and aft eight inches to benefit either passenger or cargo space. The only powertrain was a 185-hp 3.4-liter V-6 and five-speed automatic transmission. Available features included ABS and curtain side airbags.

Equinox joined Chevy's two existing midsize SUVs, the TrailBlazer and Blazer. The TrailBlazer added available curtain side airbags for '05, and the optional V-8 adopted GM's Displacement On Demand feature, which automatically deactivates four cylinders under light load to save fuel. Still on the midsize SUV docket was the Blazer, but it was in its final year and only the two-door version was sold to retail customers; four-doors were offered exclusively to fleets.

Also new for 2005 was the Uplander "Crossover Sport Van." Uplander was essentially the old extended-length, seven-passenger Venture minivan with a more prominent nose that was intended to add SUV flavor to the styling. Front-wheel drive was standard, and those models offered the Stabilitrak antiskid system as an option. GM's Versatrak AWD was also optional, as were front side airbags. The only powertrain offered was a 200-hp 3.5-liter V-6 and automatic transmission. Chevy's other minivan, the Astro, saw no changes in what would prove to be its final year.

Two pickups received some interesting powertrain changes. The Silverado added a "mild" Hybrid model, which was an extended-cab short bed with 2- or 4-wheel drive and a 5.3-liter V-8. The engine would shut off after coming to a stop and an electric motor would start it up again automatically, though it didn't aid in powering the vehicle. The motor/generator also provided 120-volt "household" current for running electrical appliances such as power saws, making it particularly valuable at job sites.

Of perhaps more significance, however, was the new V-8 found under the hood of the unique SSR convertible pickup. Replacing a 300-hp 5.3 was a stout 390-hp 6.0, essentially the same engine found in the Corvette. Of equal importance was the newly available six-speed manual transmission, with the previous four-speed automatic available as an option.

Changes to the remainder of the lineup were fairly minor. The Avalanche added an optional navigation system, as did the Tahoe and Suburban. Regular-length 12-passenger 3500 Express vans could be ordered with the Stabilitrak antiskid system previously available only on extended-length 15-passenger versions, and the Colorado compact pickup added an Xtreme décor package that included bodyside cladding and 18-inch wheels.

Larger available engines highlighted changes to several models in Chevy's **2006** truck lineup. Foremost among these was a Corvette-based 395-hp 6.0-liter V-8 that powered a new SS version of the regular-length TrailBlazer, which also came with automatic transmission, sport suspension,

20-inch wheels, and unique trim in either rear- or all-wheel-drive form. The Suburban 1500 LTZ model could be newly ordered with a 335-hp 6.0-liter V-8, and the Uplander added an optional 240-hp 3.9-liter V-6 to the existing 200-hp 3.5. Uplanders could also be equipped with new second-row side airbags. Express 2500 and 3500 full-size vans got a newly optional 250-hp 6.6-liter turbodiesel. Changes to other '06 models were minimal.

Redesigned big pickups were the big news for **2007.** While the light-duty 1999-2006 generation Silverado carried over for 2007 as the Silverado Classic, the redesigned Silverado was slightly longer and wider and now offered curtain side airbags and an antiskid system. Engine choices remained a 4.3-liter V-6 and V-8s of 4.8, 5.3, and 6.0 liters; the 5.3 offered versions with Active Fuel Management cylinder deactivation (formerly called Displacement On Demand) and E85 capability, while the 6.0 offered 367 hp. Buyers had a choice of two dashboard/interior trim variations called Pure Pickup and Luxury Inspired.

The same held for Heavy-duty pickups. A "Classic" model carried over, while the redesigned Silverado HD dropped the formerly optional 8.1-liter V-8 but offered a stronger 365-hp Duramax turbodiesel engine along with a standard six-speed automatic transmission.

Sharing the same new styling and mechanicals that graced the Silverado were the Avalanche, Tahoe, and Suburban. All were now available with curtain side airbags.

Resurrecting the Panel Delivery idea to the 2007

Chevrolet lineup was a new version of the company's HHR compact, four-door, front-wheel-drive "retro-styled" wagon. Called—appropriately—the HHR Panel, it had just two seats and featured blanked-out rear side windows and rear quarter windows that were perfect for displaying a company's logo.

Other truck models received only minor changes. Both the four- and five-cylinder engines in the Colorado grew slightly, now being a 185-hp 2.9-liter four and a 242-hp 3.5-liter five. Equinox got a new dashboard layout and standard antiskid system, while the TrailBlazer lost its extended-length seven-passenger version. Uplander gave up its optional AWD system but got the formerly optional 3.9-liter V-6 as standard, and the big Express van gained a 5.3-liter V-8 that could run on E85.

Powertrain changes and added standard safety features marked **2008** for Chevy's truck lineup. Headlining the powertrain news was the Tahoe Hybrid. It mated a 320-hp 6.0-liter V-8 with a "2-Mode" transmission incorporating a pair of motor/generators that assisted the V-8 during acceleration and recharged the battery pack under deceleration. Meanwhile, the Equinox gained a Sport version with a 264-hp 3.6-liter V-6, and the Silverado HD offered a version of its optional 6.6-liter turbodiesel that could run on biodiesel fuel.

On the safety front, Avalanche, TrailBlazer, and the Express van got standard curtain side airbags. Colorado, Silverado, and Uplander returned virtually unchanged, though the last was in its final model year.

Chevy added a larger midsize SUV to its lineup for **2009** that effectively replaced the Uplander minivan. Called the Traverse, it offered seating for up to eight passengers, front- or all-wheel drive, a 3.6-liter V-6 of 281-288 hp, and a six-speed automatic transmission. Its list of standard safety features included ABS, antiskid system, front side airbags, and curtain side airbags. Other SUV changes were subtle. There were no changes of note to the Equinox, TrailBlazer lost its 5.3-liter V-8 option, and the Tahoe and Suburban gained a standard six-speed automatic transmission and optional backup camera that displayed its image on both the inside rearview mirror and the optional navigation-system screen.

Aside from a Silverado Hybrid that shared its gas/electric powertrain with the Tahoe Hybrid, changes to pickups were minor. Standard Silverados got a six-speed automatic transmission and an optional 403-hp 6.2-liter V-8. Avalanche also got the six-speed, and an antiskid system was offered on some Silverado HD models. A notable change to the Colorado was the addition of a 300-hp 5.3-liter V-8 as an option.

Truck sales continued to grow during the early years of the new millennium and briefly surpassed those of cars, but rising fuel prices turned some buyers back to automobiles for personal transportation. Nevertheless, trucks remain popular choices in our mobile society, even for those who rarely use them as beasts of burden. Chevrolet trucks have been around almost as long as trucks themselves, and the Bowtie Brigade will undoubtedly be an integral part of America's landscape for many years to come.

1

2

1. The full-size Tahoe (left) and Suburban adopted the Silverado's basic styling for 2000. Buyers evidently approved, as both SUVs recorded higher calendar-year sales, even though the Tahoe lost its two-door body style. **2.** For 2001, Chevy's 3500 (one-ton) pickups, along with the 2500 HD (¾-ton) models assumed the Silverado's design. **3.** Also that year, the compact S-10 pickup gained a new crew-cab model. **4.** Not to be outdone, the related Blazer added a low-riding 2WD Xtreme version that was available on the two-door body style. **5-6.** For 2002, Chevy introduced a pickup version of the Suburban called the Avalanche. It was similar to a crew-cab pickup, except that the bed was integral with the body, and the two were separated by a removable "midgate" that allowed the 5.3-foot bed to be expanded to 8.1 feet. Avalanche came with a solid three-piece bed cover and covered bins built into the bed walls.

3

4

5

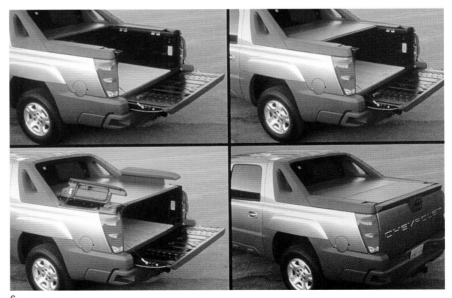

6

1

2

3

4

5

6

7

8

9

10

1. Also new for 2002 was the midsize TrailBlazer SUV. **2.** An extended-length seven-passenger TrailBlazer EXT arrived later the same year with an optional 5.3-liter V-8. **3.** The Suburban 2500 was available with Quadrasteer four-wheel steering for 2003. **4-5.** Silverado received a facelift for 2003, along with a high-performance SS model. **6.** The full-size Express van was updated for 2003 with a five-inch-longer nose and available left-side swing-out cargo doors. **7-11.** The SSR two-seat, hardtop convertible pickup arrived during the 2003 model year with an innovative folding hardtop. Based on a shortened 2-wheel-drive TrailBlazer chassis, it featured retro-flavored styling inspired by Chevy's 1948-53 trucks. Its sole powertrain was a 300-hp 5.3-liter V-8 and a four-speed automatic transmission. Prices started at $41,370. **12.** A new compact pickup arrived for 2004. Called the Colorado, it was slightly larger than an S-10 and offered two new engines: a 175-horse 2.8-liter four, and a 3.5-liter five, both based on the TrailBlazer's inline six. Regular, extended, and crew-cab models were available.

11

12

1

2

3

4

5

1. Midsize SUVs were increasingly popular, so Chevy added the Equinox "crossover" for 2005. **2.** The Venture minivan morphed into the Uplander Crossover Sport Van that same year with a boxier, SUV-flavored nose. **3.** Chevy continued to compete in the medium-duty market as well. Shown are the 2005 Kodiak C5500 (left) and C7500. **4.** A hot Corvette-powered TrailBlazer SS arrived for 2006. **5.** The small, compact-car-based HHR "trucklet" added a panel version for 2007. **6-8.** Silverado was completely redesigned for 2007. Extended-, crew-, and standard-cab models were once again available. **9-10.** The Suburban and closely related Avalanche were also redesigned for 2007. **11.** Rounding out the new '07 Chevy trucks was a fresh Tahoe.

6

7

8

9

10

11

1. A heavy-duty version of the new Silverado also arrived in 2007. For 2008 (shown), the 2500 HD LT Crew Cab was little changed. The standard engine was a 353-horsepower 6.0-liter V-8, and the only optional engine was a 6.6-liter turbodiesel rated at 365 hp. **2.** For 2008, Chevy added a Hybrid version of the full-size Tahoe SUV in rear-wheel- and all-wheel-drive versions. The hybrid drive mated a 332-hp 6.0-liter V-8 with a pair of electric motors incorporated into the transmission to create what GM dubbed its "2-Mode" system. The Tahoe Hybrid could be driven on either gas or electric propulsion or a combination of both, depending on conditions. Beyond the special powertrain, Chevy engineers added several aerodynamic tweaks including a unique front fascia along with mass-reducing items like an aluminum tailgate and lightweight passenger seats. Tahoe Hybrid prices started at $49,450.
3. For 2009, Chevy added a midsize crossover SUV called Traverse. Front-wheel drive was standard with all-wheel drive optional, and all models were powered by a 3.6-liter V-6 engine. Three-row seating was the norm, with room for seven or eight passengers depending on equipment. **4.** Chevy added a 2-Mode Hybrid version of the Silverado for 2009. It used the basic powertrain from the Tahoe Hybrid and was only available in the 1500 crew-cab body style. **5.** The big news for the compact Colorado for 2009 was the addition of an optional 300-hp 5.3-liter V-8 engine that contributed to a 6000-lb maximum towing capacity.

1

2

3

4

5

CHASSIS AND CABS

CONVENTIONAL			CAB-OVER-ENGINE			
Body Length	Weight of Body and Payload	Wheel-base	Model	Body Length	Weight of Body and Payload	Wheel-base
to 78"	1800 lb.	116"	5103	92" to 116"	11,200 lb.	110"
to 92"	2400 lb.	125¼"	5103s	92" to 116"	10,200 lb.	110"
to 116"	4900 lb.	137"	5403	120" to 168"	11,100 lb.	134"
to 116"	9500 lb.	137"	5403s	120" to 168"	10,100 lb.	134"
to 164"	9400 lb.	161"	5703	164" to 212"	11,000 lb.	158"
to 116"	11,200 lb.	137"	5703s	164" to 212"	10,000 lb.	158"
to 116"	10,200 lb.	137"				
to 164"	11,100 lb.	161"				
to 164"	10,100 lb.	161"				
to 198"	11,000 lb.	179"				

Optional equipment and special bodies and equipment, shown, are at extra cost.

BETTER THAN EVE

FOR YOUR JOB!

CHASSIS

FLAT-FACE COWL				COWL AND WINDSHIELD			
Model	Body Length	Weight of Body and Payload	Wheel-base	Model	Body Length	Weight of Body and Payload	Wh ba
3102	66″ to 84″	2200 lb.	116″	3112	66″ to 84″	2100 lb.	116
3602	72″ to 98″	2800 lb.	125¼″	3612	72″ to 98″	2700 lb.	125
3802	92″ to 124″	5300 lb.	137″	3812	92″ to 124″	5200 lb.	137
4102	92″ to 124″	9900 lb.	137″	4112	92″ to 124″	9800 lb.	137
4402	116″ to 170″	9800 lb.	161″	4412	116″ to 170″	9700 lb.	161
6102	92″ to 124″	11,600 lb.	137″	6112	92″ to 124″	11,500 lb.	137
6102s	92″ to 124″	10,600 lb.	137″	6112s	92″ to 124″	10,500 lb.	137
6402	116″ to 170″	11,500 lb.	161″	6412	116″ to 170″	11,400 lb.	161
6402s	116″ to 170″	10,500 lb.	161″	6412s	116″ to 170″	10,400 lb.	161
6502	156″ to 204″	11,400 lb.	179″	6512	156″ to 204″	11,300 lb.	179
6502s	156″ to 204″	10,400 lb.	179″	6512s	156″ to 204″	10,300 lb.	179

SCHOOL BUS CHASSIS				FORWARD-CONTROL CHAS			
3802	144″	16 pupils	137″	3742	108″ to 120″	4300 lb.	12
4502	204″	36 pupils	161″	3942	120″ to 132″	6750 lb.	13

Index